Pope Francis

Pope Francis

Matthew E. Bunson, D.Min.

Our Sunday Visitor Publishing Division
Our Sunday Visitor, Inc.
Huntington, Indiana 46750

POPE FRANCIS

Pope Francis

✠

Born Jorge Mario Bergoglio
December 17, 1936
Buenos Aires, Argentina

Entered Society of Jesus
March 11, 1958

Ordained Priest
December 13, 1969

Ordained Titular Bishop of Auca
and Auxiliary Bishop of Buenos Aires
June 27, 1992

Appointed Coadjutor Archbishop of Buenos Aires
June 3, 1997

Archbishop of Buenos Aires
February 28, 1998

Created Cardinal
February 21, 2001

Elected Pope
March 13, 2013

Prayer for Pope Francis

—————————— ✛ ——————————

Lord God,
with great joy
we give thanks for your faithful servant, Pope Francis.
Bless our Holy Father
with wisdom, zeal, and the gift of governance
as he guides your Church in peace and unity.
May his humility, simplicity, and love
inspire your people to share the Good News of Jesus Christ
as a light for the poor, the marginalized, and all the world.
Amen.

CONTENTS

———— ✠ ————

FOREWORD

⊹

O ne of the thrills of being a journalist is to be on the spot when history is being made. If journalism is the first draft of history, journalists are history's eyewitnesses. What I witnessed during two weeks in Rome covering the interregnum, conclave, and election of Pope Francis was astounding, both because much of it was unpredicted and because it began a surprising and inspiring new chapter for the Church.

Few people predicted that Cardinal Jorge Mario Bergoglio would be the next pope. It was likely true that he was the second-largest vote-getter at the 2005 conclave, though, of course, there is no official confirmation of that fact. But that was eight years ago, and the man who had been a relatively young sixty-eight was now a much older seventy-six. For this reason alone, he was not on most people's lists.

There had been much discussion about who was papabile and who was not in the weeks leading up to the conclave, with Americans on many lists for the first time, and most observers conceding that the front-runner was the Italian archbishop of Milan, Cardinal Angelo Scola.

So when Cardinal Jean-Louis Tauran announced that the new pope was "Bergoglio," the collective reaction of the crowd would be best described as optimistic puzzlement. He was to be named "Francis," they heard, which was a good sign, but who was he?

Then came those first seconds on the balcony, when he stood motionless, looking almost in shock: *Ecce homo*, behold the man. Perhaps we in the crowd were in shock as well, waiting for some sign of who our new pope would be. His first words were softly enunciated: "*Buona sera*" ("Good evening"). It was almost casual, certainly informal, yet a small sign that we were about to meet a man quite different from some of our expectations.

Think of those first moments and the other spontaneous signs he gave that revealed to us evidence of his character: He prayed for his predecessor, Benedict, "the emeritus bishop of Rome," using the basic prayers of our Catholic faith. He asked us to bless him before he blessed us. He refused to wear the more ornate papal vestments. And he insistently presented himself as the bishop and pastor of Rome.

There was humility to his very first words and actions that not only captured the imagination of the crowd in the Saint Peter's Square, but also the tens of millions watching on television.

In the days that followed, he did not so much outline a program as reveal aspects of his character. Some of these gestures — blessing a pregnant woman outside of the Basilica of Saint Mary Major, paying his own bill at the hotel where he had been staying, embracing the crippled man in Saint Peter's Square, choosing to celebrate Holy Thursday with young people in a juvenile detention center — dramatically attracted the attention of the world. It is not as if no pope had ever done these things. Yet the fact that he was at once both forceful and humble — insisting that he be able to do these things from the very beginning — entranced the media and fed the popular imagination.

At the same time, if we focus only on the empathetic gesture and the sympathetic act, we only understand part of Pope Francis. While he has not laid out his program yet — and may not for some time as he adjusts to both the Vatican and the global complexities of a world Church — there are clues to who the man is and what he considers priorities.

And the priorities of Francis begin first of all with Christ: "Christ is the Church's pastor," he told the world's media in his first audience with them. "Christ remains the center, not the Successor of Peter: Christ, Christ is the center. Christ is the fundamental point of reference, the heart of the Church." Everything flows from that realization. For if this is not true, then nothing is true. Once this is understood, then one also understands that the Church is ultimately not a political institution but a spiritual one, and that the Church is certainly not just the pope, or just the cardinals and bishops. "The Church is the People of God, the Holy People of God making its way to encounter Jesus Christ."

This is our story. It is one of encounter and journey. It is one of radical fellowship. And from this realization flow both our obligation to evangelize and our obligation to live as Christ and sacrifice as Christ.

What it means to follow Christ's footsteps in the modern world will no doubt be spelled out in more detail in the weeks and months ahead by Francis, but it is clear that he does not view the Church as simply some benign do-gooder organization, or what he described as "a charitable NGO," a nongovernmental organization like UNICEF or Oxfam. What we are challenged to do, he told the cardinals themselves in the concluding Mass of the conclave, is to carry our Cross. "When we journey without the Cross, when we build without the Cross, when we profess Christ without the Cross, we are not disciples of the Lord, we are worldly." And speaking to the most powerful men in the Catholic Church, the men who had just elected him, he added: "We may be bishops, priests, cardinals, popes, but not disciples of the Lord. My wish is that all of us, after these days of grace, will have the courage, yes, the courage, to walk in the presence of the Lord, with the Lord's cross."

There are echoes here of Saint Francis embracing the leper, of a radical Christian love that leads to laying down one's life for another. It is in this light that we are to understand his deep love for the poor, the suffering, the fallen away, those who are marginalized in all senses of the word. The AIDS sufferer, the youthful criminal, the paralytic — all of those are, in the eloquent words of Blessed Mother Teresa, Jesus in one of his more distressing disguises.

What we can expect to see, therefore, is a pope who is not a sharp departure from his predecessors, but one who will emphasize parts of the Christian message that may have become casualties of the polarization that afflicts the Church as well as secular society. He will not tolerate the false divisions that pit the Church's social teachings against the Church's doctrine. He will lead by example.

Nor will Francis be afraid to challenge the powers that be — whether cardinals or presidents. He will not abandon the Church's message of the inviolable dignity of all human life, from conception to natural death, but he will also not be afraid to draw out the implications of this message beyond the decades-long battles over abortion, euthanasia, and infanticide. He has the courage and strength to preach truth to power, and I think we can expect no less when he challenges world leaders or pastors or ordinary Catholics in the months and years ahead.

Yet the challenge he extends to all of us will be tempered by mercy and forgiveness. He is reported to have encouraged the confessors at Saint Mary Major to always extend forgiveness to the world's pilgrims, whose confessions they hear. And when he preached without a text in the parish church of the Vatican the Sunday after his election, he preached on Jesus forgiving the adulteress and saving her from stoning. "Mercy," said Pope Francis, "is the Lord's most powerful message."

"It is not easy to entrust oneself to the mercy of God, because [His mercy] is an unfathomable abyss — but we must do it!"

And like the Lord, Pope Francis saved his harshest words for those who hold themselves above others, who look down on others.

"If we are like the Pharisee before the altar, [who said], 'Thank you, Lord, for not making me like all the other men, and especially not like that fellow at the door, like that publican' … well, then we do not know the heart of the Lord, and we shall not ever have the joy of feeling this mercy."

Who is Pope Francis? In this book, this first draft of history in the making, Matthew Bunson provides the biography, the context, and the likely path forward of our new pope. While we do not know what crises and opportunities will shape this new pontificate in the years ahead, with this book we will better understand who Francis is, this humble man called from the ends of the earth to lead the Holy People of God forward into the millennium.

— GREG ERLANDSON

INTRODUCTION

—✠—

This book is the story of two journeys.

On February 11, 2013, Pope Benedict XVI stunned the world when he announced that he was resigning the papacy and that the College of Cardinals would gather in Rome to elect his successor. From 8:00 p.m. on the evening of February 28, when the resignation took effect, the Church was without a shepherd. Over the next weeks, the Church traveled a path through the *sede vacante*, a time of suspense and also of mourning, for although Benedict had not died, the end of his pontificate was poignant.

Halfway across the world, Cardinal Jorge Mario Bergoglio, the archbishop of Buenos Aires, Argentina, prepared for his journey to Rome and the conclave. He bought a return ticket, and his friends, aghast at the state of his battered old shoes, implored him to accept the gift of a new pair. Wearing his new shoes, he set out for the Vatican.

Two journeys — one for the whole Church and another for one of her members — ended in the chapel filled with the frescoes of Michelangelo, beneath the gaze of the "Last Judgment." On March 13, the College of Cardinals elected Cardinal Bergoglio to serve as the 265th Successor of Peter. He took the name Francis.

The resignation of Pope Benedict was one of the most astonishing events in modern Church history. Papal resignations are exceedingly rare in the unbroken line of popes — the last took place in 1415. And though it seemed that Pope Benedict's departure could open the possibility of severe crisis, the Church was prepared both by her laws and traditions to provide stability and continuity even at a moment like this. The result was the election of someone who was unanticipated but who showed immediately that he was prepared to assume the weight of the papacy, to wear the Fisherman's Ring and the pallium, and to take upon himself the enormity of the Petrine ministry, which Blessed John Paul II called "the service proper to the Bishop of Rome."

In some ways, this book began not with the resignation of Pope Benedict but eight years earlier with his election. Cardinal Joseph Ratzinger was the clear favorite heading into that conclave, but the other serious candidate to emerge from among the cardinals was Jorge Mario Bergoglio. In the years after, he continued to shepherd his archdiocese with pastoral zeal, a respected leader in the Church in Latin America and within the College of Cardinals. While he did not appear on the radar of most of the media in the discussions of the so-called *papabili* following Benedict's announcement, he emerged as God's choice from his fellow cardinals.

This book covers the momentous events surrounding Pope Benedict's decision and the conclave that elected Cardinal Bergoglio, but is taken up principally with the life of Pope Francis. It includes a detailed biography of the new pope's early life, his priesthood as a Jesuit during a dark time in Argentina's history, his labors as archbishop of Buenos Aires, and finally his time as one of the most influential cardinals in Latin America and beyond. A final chapter examines the crises and opportunities that await the new pontiff and offers an analysis of what his response to those situations might be.

Pope Francis is a pontiff of many firsts, as this book makes clear. A thoroughly unforeseen pope, he has settled into the unimaginably complex and heavy role as Saint Peter's successor with an ease that many find just as surprising. He has established several key watchwords in the early days of his ministry: mercy, humility, service, authenticity. He has made gestures, large and small, that have already begun pointing to his vision for the papacy and the Church, but his greatest gesture was the first. He chose the name Francis in honor of Saint Francis of Assisi, and he did so with a deep understanding of the two most lasting legacies of *il Poverello* — a love for the poor and a commitment to reform.

Like Francis of Assisi, Pope Francis wants the Church to be poor in spirit, to be humble and Christlike in her prophetic service to the weak, the vulnerable, the forgotten, and the defenseless. But Francis of Assisi was also a reformer, one of the most significant in Church history. With other reformers of his time, such as Saint Dominic, he helped the Church recapture her apostolic zeal and be purified so that all Catholics could proclaim with joy that Jesus Christ is the Way, the Truth, and the Life.

Pope Francis's choice of name met with thunderous approval from the cardinals — and not just the three Franciscans in the conclave. They all understood the significance — Pope Francis will be a reformer but, in the tradition of *il Poverello*, that reform will be grounded in a spiritual renewal characterized by humility and mercy and intent on leading humanity to an encounter with Christ.

Francis is well aware of the obstacles to that encounter for both the rich and the poor. He lamented in an interview with EWTN in 2012 that people in developed countries worry more about their dogs than their children and spend untold amounts of money on cosmetics. More important, he argued, is the beauty of the Spirit, the beauty of the heart: "That has nothing to do with the artificial beauty of cosmetics. We wear a costume when we don't have the beauty of God." Finding Christ in such a world is daunting.

But his most vivid experiences have come in the worst slums of Argentina, where he has said Mass, baptized malnourished children, and washed and kissed the feet of drug addicts and AIDS victims. For them, sheer survival is paramount and daily existence is filled with pressing and searing distractions. An encounter with Christ seems just as remote for the poor as for the most self-absorbed sophisticate in the world's great cities.

As pontiff, Francis stands now truly as the bridge builder. His origins, his learning, and his own years of service as a pastor over a city that has some of the wealthiest residents in South America and some of the poorest has prepared him for this role. He was a shepherd to them all, and he labored to help everyone in his care encounter Christ. And now he will work to do the same for the world.

We see in the election of Pope Francis the loving and merciful hand of God's providence. As he told the reporters who had been covering the memorable events unfolding in Rome: "In everything that has occurred, the principal agent has been, in the final analysis, the Holy Spirit. He prompted the decision of Benedict XVI for the good of the Church; he guided the cardinals in prayer and in the election."

Oremus pro pontifice nostro Francisco
Dominus conservet eum,
et vivificet eum,
et beatum faciat eum in terra,
et non tradat eum
in animam inimicorum eius.

Let us pray for Francis, our Pope.
May the Lord preserve him,
and give him life,
and make him blessed upon the earth,
and deliver him not up to the will of his enemies [Ps 40:3].

— MATTHEW E. BUNSON, MARCH 23, 2013

POPE FRANCIS

⊕

A Chronology of Events

1936
✠ Dec. 17, 1936: Born in Buenos Aires, Argentina, in the Flores barrio (neighborhood) of the city to parents of Italian origin.

1953
✠ September 21, 1953: After confession, he receives an overwhelming experience of God's loving mercy that directs him toward the religious life and the priesthood.

1957
✠ He becomes severely ill with a lung infection; after a bout of pneumonia, part of his right lung is removed.

1958
✠ March 11, 1958: Enters novitiate of the Society of Jesus and begins a long period of formation.

1960
✠ March 12, 1960: Takes first vows as a member of the Society of Jesus.
✠ Studies in Chile, where he focuses on the humanities.

1961-63
✠ Studies philosophy at San Miguel Seminary, Buenos Aires.

1964-65
✠ Teaches in a high school in Santa Fe, Argentina; he teaches literature and psychology.

1966
✠ Teaches at the Colegio del Salvador, in Buenos Aires.

1967-70
✠ Studies theology at San Miguel Seminary, Argentina.

1969

✠ December 13, 1969: Ordained as a priest by Archbishop Ramón José Castellano.

1970-71

✠ Undergoes his tertianship, or third probation period of Jesuit formation, at Alcalá de Henares, Spain.

1971-73

✠ Serves as master of novices and vice chancellor, San Miguel Seminary, Argentina.

1973

✠ April 22, 1973: Takes final vows as a member of the Society of Jesus.

✠ July 31, 1973: Elected provincial of the Jesuits of Argentina; he serves until 1979.

1976-83

✠ Argentina undergoes the so-called Dirty War that brings the deaths of as many as 35,000 people.

1979-85

✠ Serves as rector of Colegio Máximo and as theology teacher.

1982

✠ Publishes *Meditaciones para religiosos* (*Meditation for Religious*).

1986

✠ Studies in Germany and completes his doctorate in theology in Freiburg; publishes *Reflexiones sobre la vida apostólica* (*Reflections on the Apostolic Life*); returns to Argentina where he serves as a teacher and spiritual director and confessor.

1992

✠ May 20, 1992: Appointed titular bishop of Auca and auxiliary bishop of Buenos Aires.

✠ June 27, 1992: Ordained titular bishop of Auca and auxiliary bishop of Buenos Aires by Cardinal Antonio Quarracino, archbishop of Buenos Aires; publishes *Reflexiones de esperanza* (*Reflections of Hope*)

1994

✠ October 2-29, 1994: Attends the Ninth Ordinary Assembly of the Synod of Bishops in Rome.

1997

✠ June 3, 1997: Appointed coadjutor archbishop of Buenos Aires.

✠ November 16-December 12, 1997: Attends the Special Assembly for America of the Synod of Bishops in Rome.

1998

✠ February 28, 1998: Becomes archbishop of Buenos Aires upon the death of Cardinal Quarracino.

2001

✠ February 21, 2001: Named to the College of Cardinals as a cardinal priest; he receives the title of S. Roberto Bellarmino.

✠ September 30-October 27, 2001: Attends the Tenth Ordinary Assembly of the Synod of Bishops in Rome and is named relator after Cardinal Edward Egan is unable to leave New York after 9/11.

✠ September 30-October 27, 2001: Attends the Tenth Ordinary Assembly of the Synod of Bishops in Rome.

2005

✠ April 18-19, 2005: Attends the conclave that elects Cardinal Joseph Ratzinger, who chooses the name Pope Benedict XVI; it is widely reported that Cardinal Bergoglio received the second highest number of votes.

✠ October 2-23, 2005: Attends the Eleventh General Ordinary Assembly of the Synod of Bishops in Rome.

✠ November 9, 2005: Elected president of the Argentinian Bishops Conference; he is reelected in 2008.

2007

✠ May 13-31, 2007: Participated in the Fifth General Conference of the Latin American Bishops Episcopate, which took place in Aparecida, Brazil; he is elected president of the commission to draft the final document.

2013

✠ March 13, 2013: Elected pope by a conclave of 115 cardinals and takes the name Francis.

✠ March 19, 2013: Inauguration Mass is held for the official start of his pontificate.

PART I

—✠—

Sede Vacante: The Vacant See

"With full freedom I declare that I renounce the ministry of Bishop of Rome, Successor of Saint Peter."

— Pope Benedict XVI, February 11, 2013

Chapter One

"AT THE END THERE WAS SILENCE"

---✠---

"Dear Brothers, I thank you most sincerely for all the love and work with which you have supported me in my ministry, and I ask pardon for all my defects."

— POPE BENEDICT XVI, FEBRUARY 11, 2013

O n the morning of February 11, 2013, the residential cardinals in Rome — those who serve in the Roman Curia and other posts in and around Rome and the Vatican City State — gathered in the ornate Consistory Hall in the Apostolic Palace of the Vatican for a planned consistory, a meeting of cardinals with Pope Benedict XVI. On the agenda was the approval of several miracles leading to the canonizations of three new saints for the Church. The meeting proceeded as normal, and the pontiff, tired, as he had been for some time, presided in his usual quiet and gentle fashion.

Once the matter at hand was concluded, the cardinals rose to receive the papal blessing. It was at that point, however, that Pope Benedict asked them to be seated, as he wished to speak to them. The puzzled cardinals took their seats, and the Holy Father quietly read a prepared text in Latin. His voice was frail:

I have convoked you to this consistory, not only for the three canonizations, but also to communicate to you a decision of great importance for the life of the Church. After having repeatedly examined my conscience before God, I have come to the certainty that my strengths, due to an advanced age, are no longer suited to an adequate exercise of the Petrine ministry. I am well aware that this ministry, due to its essential spiritual nature, must be carried out not only with words and deeds, but no less with prayer and suffering. However, in today's world, subject to so many rapid changes and shaken by questions of deep relevance for the life of faith, in order to govern the barque of Saint Peter and proclaim the Gospel, both strength of mind and body are necessary, strength which in the last few months, has deteriorated in me to the extent that I have had to recognize my incapacity to adequately fulfill the ministry entrusted to me.

For this reason, and well aware of the seriousness of this act, with full freedom I declare that I renounce the ministry of Bishop of Rome, Successor of Saint Peter, entrusted to me by the cardinals on 19 April 2005, in such a way, that as from 28 February 2013, at 20:00 hours, the See of Rome, the See of Saint Peter, will be vacant and a conclave to elect the new Supreme Pontiff will have to be convoked by those whose competence it is.

Dear Brothers, I thank you most sincerely for all the love and work with which you have supported me in my ministry, and I ask pardon for all my defects. And now, let us entrust the Holy Church to the care of Our Supreme Pastor, Our Lord Jesus Christ, and implore his holy Mother Mary, so that she may assist the cardinal fathers with her maternal solicitude, in electing a new Supreme Pontiff. With regard to myself, I wish to also devotedly serve the Holy Church of God in the future through a life dedicated to prayer.

As it happened, the moment was captured on the Vatican's own television network, CTV, with the startled look of the Apostolic Almoner (who distributes aid in the name of the pope from the Office of Papal Charities), Archbishop Guido Pozzi, revealing the shock that gripped the room. At the end of the pope's statement, Cardinal Angelo Sodano, the Dean of the College of Cardinals, read a prepared text — he was, in fact, one of the few Vatican officials to know ahead of time the stunning statement the pope was about to give:

Your Holiness, beloved and revered Successor of Peter,

Your moving message has resounded in this room like a lightning bolt in a calm sky.

We've listened to you with a sense of shock, rather in total disbelief. In your words we noticed the great affection that you have always had for the Holy Church of God, for this Church that you have loved so much.

Allow me to tell you, in the name of this apostolic cenacle — the College of Cardinals — in the name of your dear collaborators, let me tell you that we are closer to you than ever before, just as we have been in these eight luminous years of your pontificate.

On 19 April 2005, if I remember right, at the end of the conclave, I asked you, with trembling voice after all our years together, "Do you accept your canonical election as Supreme Pontiff?" And you did not take long — albeit with trepidation — to respond by saying that you accepted with trust in the Lord and in the maternal intercession of Mary, Mother of the Church.

With Mary, that day you gave your "yes," and so began your luminous pontificate with the plow of continuity, that continuity of which you have spoken to us so often in the history of the Church — continuity with your 265 predecessors in the Chair of Peter, in the course of two thousand years of history, from the Apostle Peter, humble fisherman of Galilee, right through to the great popes of the last century, from Saint Pius X to Blessed John Paul II.

Holy Father, before February 28 — the day which, as you have said, you seek to put the word "*fine*" [the end] over your service as pontiff, one given with so much love, with humility — before February 28, we will have a way to better express our feelings, so will many pastors and faithful throughout the world, as will so many people of good will along with the authorities of many countries. In this month to come, too, we will have the joy of hearing your shepherd's voice on Ash Wednesday, then on Thursday, with the clergy of Rome, in the Angelus of these Sundays, at the Wednesday audiences; there will thus be many opportunities still to hear your fatherly voice. . . .

Even beyond these, your mission will continue onward: you have said that you will always be close to us with your witness and your prayers. Sure as the stars in the sky always continue to shine, so the star of your pontificate will always shine in our midst.

We are close to you, Holy Father — bless us.

One of the witnesses to the papal announcement, longtime Vatican official Cardinal Francis Arinze of Nigeria, the prefect emeritus of the Congregation for Divine Worship and Discipline of the Sacraments, described the scene to Catholic News Service: "As the pope's meaning became unambiguous, the cardinals looked at one another in silence, in surprise. At the end there was silence."

"After the pope left the room, we did not go away," the cardinal said. "We got together in little groups, as it were, each one asking, 'What has happened?' But there was no doubt about esteem for the Holy Father, for his courage and his love for the church." "It may well be that his health is not as strong as I thought," Cardinal Arinze said. "He loves the Church so much that he thinks it's better for the Church that he leave and another person take over this heavy burden. I haven't any doubt about his wisdom. He doesn't rush. He is not rash. He is gentle. But he's also clearheaded and firm."

The scene in the room was also described vividly by the Vatican newspaper, *L'Osservatore Romano*, in its February 12 edition, as one of "dismay, surprise, amazement, and emotion."

The Vatican Press Office soon made the official announcement, but it scarcely needed to do so as word spread within minutes beyond the Apostolic Palace across the Vatican City State and then Rome.

The international media frenzy had begun . . .

And so Pope Benedict XVI would become the first pontiff to resign in 598 years. The last time a pontiff had voluntarily renounced the papacy was in 1415 when Pope Gregory XII stepped down to clear the way for an end to the Great Western Schism that had divided the Church since 1378. Several facts were obvious. The first was that Benedict had indeed reached the decision freely and in good conscience. Second, the number of officials who were privy to his deliberations was very small and included only his most key advisers, including his private secretary, Archbishop Georg Gänswein. He had informed the Dean of the College, Cardinal Sodano, not long before making the announcement, and so the papal action remained a genuine secret. As will be seen, there had been rumors about the pope's health swirling for some time in the Vatican, but the final decision to renounce the papacy was held closely and kept safe until Benedict's actual declaration.

✠

Though 78 when he was elected pope in 2005, he set out to meet his people — and they were of all faiths — all over the world. He visited the religiously threatened — Jews, Muslims, and Christians in the war-torn Middle East, the desperately poor in Africa, and the world's youth gathered to meet him in Australia, Germany, and Spain....

Those who met him, heard him speak, and read his clear, profound writings found themselves moved and changed. In all he said and did he urged people everywhere to know and have a personal encounter with Jesus Christ.

— CARDINAL TIMOTHY DOLAN OF NEW YORK

The shock in the consistory was itself sufficient to confirm the success in maintaining discretion, as was the genuine surprise the announcement elicited from the world's cardinals who would be gathering in Rome to choose a new Supreme Pontiff. The Italian Cardinal Angelo Scola of Milan, it was reported, refused at first to believe the news when an official called him from Rome.

The first and most immediately difficult task fell to the Vatican Press spokesperson, Fr. Federico Lombardi, director of the Holy See Press Office, who went before the clamoring international press corps and sought to provide some clarity. He commented in the Vatican Press Office and on Vatican Radio:

Among the reasons for the pope's resignation, as he noted in his own words, are the circumstances of today's world that, in relation to the past, are particularly difficult, both because of the speed as well as the number of events and problems that arise that, therefore, need a vigor, perhaps stronger than in the past. It is a vigor that the pope says he has felt diminish in him in recent months.

He continued:

The phrase: "well aware of the seriousness of this act, with full freedom I declare that I renounce the ministry of Bishop of Rome,

Successor of Saint Peter," is very significant. This is the formal declaration, which is important from a juridical point of view. In paragraph 2 of canon 332 of the *Code of Canon Law*, we read: "Should it happen that the Roman Pontiff resigns from his office, it is required for validity that the resignation be freely made and properly manifested, but it is not necessary that it be accepted by anyone." The two fundamental points are, therefore, freedom and due manifestation. Freedom and public manifestation — and the consistory in which the pope manifested his will is public.

Lombardi then provided a few further details as to the pope's last weeks in office:

Benedict XVI will continue to fully carry out his functions and his service until 28 February at 8:00 p.m. From that moment on, the situation of *Sede Vacante* will begin, regulated, from a legal and canonical standpoint, by the texts referring to *Sede Vacante* in the *Code of Canon Law* and the apostolic constitution *Universi dominici gregis* by John Paul II, regarding the *Sede Vacante* of the Apostolic See.

Lombardi concluded:

Personally, I received the announcement of the pope's resignation with great admiration, for its great valor, for the Holy Father's freedom of spirit and great concern for the responsibility of his ministry. Benedict XVI has offered us a great witness of spiritual freedom, of great wisdom in regard to Church government in today's world.

The few facts proved insufficient to the press that had itself been caught completely unprepared for the events of the day. Members of the press persisted in their questions, with one demand the most pressing: What exactly prompted Benedict XVI to renounce the papacy?

The Pope's Health

From virtually the moment he announced he was stepping down, Pope Benedict XVI's motives became the subject of wild theorizing by many in the press. There was an almost pathological unwillingness on the part of some in the media to accept the notion that he might have

✠

CAN POPES RESIGN?

Catholics and non-Catholics alike are familiar with the reality that popes typically stay in office until death. The inevitability of a pontificate coming to an end played out with poignancy in 2005 with the last weeks and final passing of Blessed John Paul II. Less familiar and slightly more unnerving is the papal privilege of resigning or renouncing the papacy.

In truth, the laws of the Church are clear on this. The *Code of Canon Law* states: "Should it happen that the Roman Pontiff resigns from his office, it is required for validity that the resignation be freely made and properly manifested, but it is not necessary that it be accepted by anyone" (Canon 332, subsection 2).

What does that mean?

A pope wields supreme authority in the Church. As such, there is in effect no other authority in the Church to receive his resignation. For example, it is not as though the College of Cardinals would gather and "reluctantly accept" the resignation.

Two things are needed for a papal resignation to be valid. The first is that the pontiff act in full freedom. In other words, that he not step down by an act of coercion or under threat. The second requirement is that his resignation be made manifest, or in a public fashion.

Pope Benedict made certain that he met both of these requirements when he announced his resignation on February 11.

been resigning because of his health. That day and in the days to follow, his claims of declining strength were dismissed as mere cover for a variety of theories: that he was being driven from the papal throne by scandals in the Vatican, by his despair over "divisions" in the Church, and especially by his "failure" to deal with the sexual abuse crisis. The facts as they were soon revealed should have ended the speculation.

Benedict had accepted election to the papacy only with great reluctance in 2005. As Cardinal Joseph Ratzinger, he had tried to retire several times during the pontificate of John Paul II, but his predecessor would not hear of it, especially as John Paul considered him one of his closest collaborators in the Petrine ministry. Toward the end of his life, Pope John Paul called him "my trusted friend." By the 1990s, according to Cardinal Ratzinger's own statements, he was ready to retire, but in a conversation he had with the pope, John Paul said to him: "We're both getting old, Joseph. We must continue to work together."

As Cardinal Ratzinger related in an EWTN interview prior to his election, he had wanted to step down in 1991, 1996, and 2001, with the hope of returning to his writing and studies, in much the same way as had Cardinal Carlo Martini, the former Archbishop of Milan and noted biblical scholar.

By early 2005, then-Cardinal Ratzinger was preparing for the end of the John Paul pontificate. He was planning to enter retirement in Regensburg, Germany, and even went so far as to sell his automobile. With John Paul II's passing, Ratzinger, as Dean of the College of Cardinals, was tasked with working closely with the then-camerlengo, Spanish Cardinal Eduardo Martinez Somalo, who served as chamberlain of the Roman Church and was thus responsible for overseeing the conclave to elect a new pope.

Ratzinger delivered a memorable homily at John Paul's funeral on April 8, before the 164 members of the College of Cardinals, the patriarchs of the Eastern Catholic Churches, representatives of 169 countries, and more than 500,000 people who had packed St. Peter's Square and the Via della Conciliazione. It was, quite literally, the largest funeral in human history.

By the start of the conclave, the list of *papabili* (papal candidates) had grown much shorter. And Ratzinger was now the clear favorite. It was a statement of the trust given to him by the majority of cardinals that only four ballots were apparently needed to secure his election on April 19.

He was 78 years old, the oldest pope chosen by the College of Cardinals in 300 years. It was generally acknowledged, however, that despite a few minor medical issues, the new pope enjoyed sound health. In 1991, while still a cardinal, he had suffered a mild hemorrhagic stroke that briefly damaged his eyesight, but he had recovered fully. It was assumed at the time of his election that he would reign as pope for at least five years.

There was also the issue of a pacemaker. The Vatican confirmed, after the papal resignation was announced, that Benedict had received a pacemaker some years prior to his election as pope, and that he had had a routine replacement of the batteries three months ago, although the procedure had absolutely no impact on his overall health, nor did it drive his decision to renounce the papacy.

The generally excellent health of the pope over the first years of his pontificate was apparent to observers who noted that he walked with purpose and enjoyed surprising strength even during long papal liturgies and papal travels. His durability benefited from a prudent approach to travel. Each journey included rest breaks, such as the weeklong break for the pope after the grueling flight to Australia in 2008 to take part in World Youth Day in Sydney.

The situation changed slightly in 2009. During his traditional summer vacation in the Italian Alps in July, he fell, broke his wrist, and required surgery to set it properly. Later that same year, during a Christmas Eve Mass, a mentally deranged woman jumped the barrier inside St. Peter's Basilica, grabbed the pontiff by his vestments, and dragged him to the ground. He was unharmed — his close friend Cardinal Roger Etchegeray, caught in the melee, was not so fortunate and broke his hip — but the incident raised concern among the pope's security staff.

I have no doubt that what [Pope Benedict] has done is really in keeping with his character, because he is a person of courage, who does what he sees is right and is not afraid of what people will say, what people will do — that's what he has shown right through his pontificate....

He had the courage to do something that no other pope has done for the last 600 years.

He has taught us that all authority is for service.

— Cardinal Oswald Gracias, archbishop of Bombay, India

Observers began to note that Benedict started to slow down incrementally over the next two years. He was more deliberate in taking the stairs during papal liturgies, and he started to rely on his masters of ceremony, especially Msgr. Guido Marini, to provide him a steady hand during parts of the Mass. And then, in the fall of 2011, those in attendance at St. Peter's Basilica for a liturgy were shocked to watch the pope transported the length of the basilica in the device that had last been used to assist John Paul II at the end of his pontificate.

The Vatican Press Office explained that the transport had been put into use again in order to spare the energies of the pope, not because of any specific medical problem. The stories soon circulated that Pope Benedict was indeed suffering from a form of arthritis. But more lasting was the image that had been left of the pope utilizing a transport device last seen in the twilight of a previous pontificate. New rumors followed at a steady pace. In September 2011, the Italian journalist Antonio Socci wrote in the *Libero* newspaper that Vatican officials were increasingly concerned the pope was considering resignation, possibly when he turned 85 in April the next year. That did not happen, but the scrutiny of his health intensified during Benedict's March 2012 trip to Mexico and Cuba, when he seemed exhausted during long stretches in the sweltering heat. Later, the Vatican confirmed that while in Mexico he fell and hit his head while searching for a light switch in a dark room, but the injury was minor and had no impact on the trip.

The journey to Mexico and Cuba was followed by a brief visit to Lebanon in September in what proved to be the last trip of his pontificate. Stories soon began that he was increasingly infirm, that he used a wheelchair to get around the Apostolic Palace, and that he was also supposedly suffering from cancer. The truth of these claims was never verified, but by the time of the grueling Christmas liturgies, he was struggling. There was an especially poignant moment when Benedict met with young people belonging to the Taizé Movement on December 30 and was trying to summon the energy needed to complete his address to the 40,000 who had come to see him.

German journalist Peter Seewald added some additional medical details as well. After seeing Benedict some ten weeks before the resignation, he informed the Daily Mail that the pontiff's vision had declined severely in one eye, and he was exhausted. Further reports pointed to marked decline in the pope's hearing.

By the start of the New Year, there were those in Rome who were expressing a certain pessimism about the pope's long-term durability. But the idea of a resignation was not raised again as it had been a year before, and the day-to-day routine of the Holy See continued on in a seemingly normal fashion for weeks. The pontiff, however, had completed his own deliberations and was already moving toward renunciation.

HISTORY OF PAPAL RESIGNATIONS

Contrary to early media reports, Benedict was not the third pontiff to resign the papacy. In truth, the exact number is not known with certainty because some pontiffs stepped down in the face of exile or deposition by external forces, such as at the hands of the Byzantine emperors who tried to meddle in the life of the Church. The following are some of the popes who are known to have resigned:

Pontian (r. 230-235) was the first pope to resign. Arrested during the severe persecution of Christians under Emperor Maximinus Thrax, he was sent to the mines on Sardina. In order to make it possible for his successor to be chosen, he resigned on September 28, 235.

John XVIII (1003-1009) reigned briefly during a difficult time for the papacy owing to the grasping ambitions of the Roman nobles, especially the Crescentii family. According to the records of the time, he resigned and spent his remaining days in a monastery.

Benedict IX was pope three times between 1032 and 1048. The era was a dark one, and he was in turn removed from the papal throne, returned, resigned, returned, and was finally deposed in favor of the briefly reigning pontiff Damasus II and then the reforming Pope Leo IX.

Celestine V (1294) resigned after less than a year as pope.

Gregory XII (1406-1415) resigned to end the Great Western Schism.

The Pope's Plans

According to *L'Osservatore Romano*, Pope Benedict had reached the decision to resign after his journey to Mexico and Cuba in spring 2012. That was confirmed in a press conference held on February 13 by Greg Burke, a senior Vatican communications adviser. "What's interesting is how long ago this decision was made, shortly after the pope's trip to Cuba, which was in March of last year," said Burke.

The topic had been raised in general much earlier, however. In 2010, the Holy Father gave a revealing interview to Peter Seewald. Published as *Light of the World: The Pope, the Church, and the Signs of the Times* (Ignatius Press, 2010), the book included Benedict's answers to two specific questions regarding a decision to resign.

First, Seewald asked whether, in difficult situations that might weigh on the pontificate then in progress, the pope would consider resigning. Benedict responded: "When the danger is great one must not run away. For that reason, now is certainly not the time to resign. Precisely at a time like this one must stand fast and endure the difficult situation. That is my view. One can resign at a peaceful moment or when one simply cannot go on. But one must not run away from danger and say that someone else should do it."

Second, Seewald asked: "Is it possible then to imagine a situation in which you would consider a resignation by the pope appropriate?" The Holy Father responded: "Yes. If a pope clearly recognizes that he is no longer physically, psychologically, and spiritually capable of handing the duties of his office, then he has a right and, under some circumstances, also an obligation to resign." (*Light of the World*, pp. 29-30.)

In an article on February 18, 2013, for the German weekly magazine *Focus*, that was also covered by Catholic News Service, Seewald wrote that in August 2012, while at the papal summer residence of Castel Gandolfo, Benedict had told him that his strength was diminishing. Seewald then asked the pontiff how much more could be expected for the rest of his papacy. Benedict replied: "From me? From me, not much more. I am an old man and my strength is running out. And I think what I have done is enough." Asked again about resignation, Benedict responded: "That depends to what extent my physical strength will compel me to."

The question of stepping down played out, of course, within the wider context of the final years of the pontificate of Pope John Paul II.

In his interview with EWTN before his election, then-Cardinal Ratzinger was asked why he chose to remain at work for Pope John Paul II. What compelled him to stay was the example of the Holy Father. As he put it in the interview:

> Seeing the suffering Pope, I cannot say to the Pope, "I will retire. I will write my books.". . . . Seeing him, how he is giving himself, I have to continue. . . . His suffering is in communion with the suffering of Christ, and perhaps with his suffering we can better understand that the suffering of Christ has redeemed the world — in giving himself in suffering, giving up something, giving up some activities sometime, but that really himself is the presence of the force of the deeper dimensions of human beings. We can learn from him that suffering and the gift of himself is an essential gift we need in our time.

Joseph Ratzinger accepted election to the papacy as Benedict XVI as a powerful act of service to the Church. By then he had been part of the inner circle of the late pontiff for most of John Paul's pontificate. He had grown old in the service of the pope and had dealt with innumerable crises over the decades. He had watched John Paul II grow old as well, watched him decline in strength and capacity, and watched him finally be rendered virtually silent and immobile by heartbreaking infirmities, Parkinson's disease, and the sheer weight of injuries and time.

Looking back on the quote in his interview with EWTN, it is possible to focus on the line "an essential gift we need in our time."

Pope John Paul II served as an icon of suffering, of how an individual can conform to Christ's cross to the very end. It was a powerful lesson for the Church and the world. Benedict, too, has given an equally powerful lesson, offering his entire life, his gifts, his talents, his energies to Christ and his Church. He had served as a priest, a theologian — one of the greatest theologians of the twentieth century — a bishop, an archbishop, a cardinal, and finally as Pope Benedict XVI. Having made his life a gift, in the end he offered up one last gift to the Church by renouncing the papacy.

Cardinal Arinze, in his interview with Catholic News Service, touched on this when he said that he hoped Pope Benedict's decision to resign would

> help many to get more mature in our faith . . . help all of us to be deeper in our faith, to be also, let us say, less sentimental. Our faith is not on the pope, it is on Christ who is the foundation of the Church. The pope is a servant. Indeed, one of his titles is "servant of the servants of God.". . . . So his act yesterday was like saying, "I am a servant. I think another servant should come on."

The pope's resignation "can also be a very good example for all of us," Cardinal Arinze said.

> Not only bishops. There are politicians, there are heads of state, there are heads of government who refuse to yield office even when doing so would serve the common good.
>
> So the pope's action yesterday could, we'll hope, deliver a lesson to such, whether in the church or the state or a university or a corporation. Anyone in authority is there to serve.

How significant once again were Benedict's words on the evening of April 19, when he stood upon the loggia of St. Peter's Basilica immediately after his election and said:

> Dear Brothers and Sisters,
>
> After the great Pope John Paul II, the cardinals have chosen me — a simple, humble worker in the vineyard of the Lord.
>
> It consoles me that the Lord knows how to work and to act even with inadequate instruments. So, above all, I entrust myself to your prayers.
>
> In the joy of the risen Lord, trusting in his unfailing help, let us move forward, that the Lord will help us and Mary, his Most Holy Mother, might be by our side.

Benedict XVI and Celestine V

Pope Benedict also provided further insight into his possible intentions over the course of the last several years when he spoke about one of his predecessors, Pope Saint Celestine V, who renounced the papacy in 1294.

In April 2009, Benedict visited the central Italian town of Aquila. While there, he stopped and prayed at the tomb of Celestine in the Basilica Santa Maria di Collemaggio. He then placed upon the tomb his pallium, the white woolen band of cloth adorned with red crosses that is worn by metropolitan archbishops and the pope himself, which represents their authority. The gesture was followed the next year by a visit to the Cathedral of Sulmona, in Aquila, in central Italy. While there, the pope prayed before the relics of Pope Celestine and gave a talk to the young people who had gathered to see him. He said in part:

> How does one recognize God's call? Well, the secret of the vocation lies in the capacity for and joy of distinguishing, listening to, and obeying his voice. But to do this it is necessary to accustom our hearts to recognizing the Lord and to having an awareness of him as a Person who is close to me and loves me. . . . It is important to learn to live . . . moments of inner silence in order to hear the Lord's voice. . . .
>
> And this is true both before the decision — that is, at the time of deciding and setting out — and afterwards, if one wants to be faithful and to persevere on the way. Saint Peter Celestine was first and foremost this: a man of listening, of inner silence, a man of prayer, a man of God.
>
> And here I would like to say something else . . . true prayer is not at all foreign to reality. If prayer should alienate you, remove you from your real life, be on your guard it would not be true prayer! On the contrary, dialogue with God is a guarantee of truth, of truth with ourselves and with others and hence of freedom. . . .
>
> Saint Celestine V . . . was able to act according to his conscience in obedience to God, hence without fear and with great courage even in difficult moments such as those linked to his brief pontificate, not fearing to lose his dignity but knowing that it consists in existing in truth. And the guarantee of truth is God. Those who follow him have no fear, not even of denying

themselves, of giving up their own ideas, for, as Saint Teresa of Ávila said, "Those who have God lack nothing". . . .

Another badge [distinctive sign] of the Christian: he is never an individualist. Perhaps you will say to me: but if we look, for example, at Saint Peter Celestine, in his choice of the hermitical life might there not have been individualism or an escape from responsibility? This temptation does of course exist. But in the experiences approved by the Church, the solitary life of prayer and penance is always at the service of the community, open to others, it is never in opposition to the community's needs.

WHO WAS POPE SAINT CELESTINE V?

Pietro da Morrone was Italian by birth and entered the Benedictines at the age of seventeen. Drawn to even greater austerity, he withdrew to Monte Morrone in Abruzzi where he adopted a hermit's life. There, with a group of supporters, he established what was to become the Celestine order. Renowned for his remarkable asceticism, he was elected pope at the age of eighty in order to end a gridlock in the conclave and to fill the papacy after a vacancy of some two years. When informed of his election, he expressed amazement and considerable reluctance. Convinced to accept, however, he was consecrated at Aquila with the name Celestine.

Untrained to be pontiff and ill-suited for the office, Celestine soon realized he should have refused. Aware of the damage he was doing to the Church, Celestine resigned before a consistory of cardinals at Naples. A few days later, Boniface VIII was elected. The new pontiff ordered Celestine to be taken into custody to prevent his misuse by scheming opponents. The onetime Vicar of Christ was imprisoned at the castle of Fumone, near Anagni, where he died on May 19, 1296. When taken to his cell, he reportedly commented: "I have wanted nothing in my life but a cell, and a cell they have given me."

Celestine was canonized by Clement V in 1313. Dante placed Celestine at the entrance to hell in the *Divine Comedy*, referring to him with the line "him who made, through cowardice, the great refusal."

The Place of Retirement

By the afternoon of February 11, details about where the pope would be headed from the time of his official renunciation were clear. The Vatican Press Office informed the eager media that on February 28 he would meet with the gathered members of the College of Cardinals. He would then depart the Apostolic Palace for Castel Gandolfo, where he would reside for the duration of the *sede vacante* while a permanent place of residence was finished within the Vatican City State. Where that would be was also revealed: the monastic retreat of the Mater Ecclesiae, a small monastery in the Vatican gardens.

Pope John Paul II founded the monastery in 1992 to serve as a place for contemplative life within the Vatican, and it was given to the Benedictine nuns and members of the Visitation order. The entire compound has four levels, including a section for the cloistered nuns, a chapel, choir, library, gallery, common areas with a dining room, pantry, kitchen, infirmary, and an office-studio. There are also twelve monastic cells. Outside, there is a large vegetable garden that boasts peppers, tomatoes, zucchini, cabbage, lemons, and oranges that have regularly been used for the papal table. Benedict XVI had visited the compound repeatedly and said Mass in the convent chapel there in 2005, 2006, and 2009.

It was announced that here is where Benedict had chosen to spend his last days.

By the end of the day on February 11, cardinals from all over the world had issued statements on the event. It was the first glimmer of the days and weeks to come, and it revealed the degree to which they had all been caught by surprise. As it happened, the announcement merely opened the door for one of the most tumultuous pre-conclave periods in the modern history of the Church.

One last event that evening was much discussed by the media. A rainstorm passed over the Eternal City, and in the brief tempest the dome of St. Peter's was struck several times by lightning. It seemed a fitting symbol for the day.

Chapter Two

"I WILL SIMPLY BE A PILGRIM"

---✠---

"And among you, among the College of Cardinals, there is also the future pope, to whom, here today, I already promise my unconditional reverence and obedience."

— POPE BENEDICT XVI, TO THE COLLEGE OF CARDINALS, FEBRUARY 28, 2013

By the morning of February 12, 2013, in Rome, the world's media had descended in full force on the Eternal City and the Vatican Press Office as reporters from every corner of the globe scrambled for details about the impending papal resignation, the pope's final two-week schedule, and the myriad details of his life after February 28. The Vatican itself began preparations for what it knew would be massive crowds that would be hoping to attend Benedict's last public appearances.

The assumptions were proven entirely correct the next day when the Holy Father presided over the Ash Wednesday penitential services. Tens of thousands of pilgrims arrived at the basilica to say farewell to the pope, and his last formal public homily proved an emotional one. The pope declared:

> Today, Ash Wednesday, we begin a new Lenten journey, a journey that lasts forty days and leads us towards the joy of Easter, the victory of life over death. Following the ancient Roman tradition of the Lenten stations, we are gathered today for the celebration of the Eucharist. Traditionally, the first station is held in the Basilica of Santa Sabina on the Aventine Hill. Circumstances have suggested that we gather in the Vatican basilica.
>
> This evening we meet in great numbers around the tomb of the Apostle Peter, also to beg his intercession for the Church's path forward at this particular moment, renewing our faith in

the Chief Pastor, Christ the Lord. For me it is a fitting occasion to thank everyone, especially the faithful of the Diocese of Rome, as I prepare to conclude my Petrine ministry, and to ask for a special remembrance in your prayers.

Catholic Reaction

Benedict's decision to step down provoked a variety of reactions from across the Catholic world. A sampling reveals the intensity of feeling in the wake of the resignation.

Noted Vaticanista (a journalist who specializes in the Holy See) Andrea Tornielli wrote in the February 12 issue of *La Stampa*, an Italian daily newspaper:

> Had the "cross" of his pontificate become too much to bear? Absolutely, otherwise the elderly Bavarian theologian would not have resorted to taking such a drastic decision, a first in Church history, given that none of the extremely rare cases of resignations presented in the two millennia that preceded his are comparable to this. But the pope's gesture cancels out what he said in his first speech to cardinals in the Sistine Chapel after his election, about the fact that a pope must "make Christ's light shine . . . not his own". . . .
>
> In a way his gesture "relativizes" the Roman Catholic papacy. The pope is who he is because he is the Bishop of Rome. Bishops are required to hand their resignation in at the age of 75 and become accustomed to the idea of having "emeritus" status. This is not the case with the pope, and obviously an emeritus pope living in the Vatican is a burden to any of his successors.
>
> And yet despite these difficulties, people seem to forget that by requesting that his flaws be forgiven and by admitting that it was impossible for him to carry on his ministry, Benedict XVI presents himself as an example of great Christian realism. The "ministers" serving the Church are just men, and they are fragile. From the figure that occupies the Throne of Peter right down to the last priest.

Francis Rocca, in his analysis for Catholic News Service, saw the resignation as predictable in hindsight, but not for the reasons that most people thought.

Many people today associate unexpected resignations with scandal or crisis. In the immediate aftermath of Pope Benedict's announcement there was predictable speculation that he might be stepping down under pressure of some grave problem in the Church, perhaps one yet to be revealed.

But if Pope Benedict declined to resign at the height of the controversy over clerical sex abuse in late winter and early spring of 2010, when some accused him of personally mishandling cases of pedophile priests in Germany and the United States, it is hard to imagine what sort of crisis he might deem disturbing enough to resign over now. . . .

Rocca suggests:

Pope Benedict may have judged the eve of Lent a particularly good moment to announce his resignation since, as the Vatican spokesman, Jesuit Fr. Federico Lombardi, told reporters at a briefing shortly afterward, the timing practically ensures that the church will have a new pope by Easter. . . . Fr. Lombardi told reporters that Pope Benedict will retire to a monastery inside the walls of Vatican City, where he will dedicate himself to study and prayer. . . . Asked whether the presence of a living former pope would present any danger of division within the church, Fr. Lombardi replied that it would be entirely out of character for Pope Benedict to say or do anything that might undermine his successor.

That assumption seems more than fair, but Pope Benedict's humility and discretion may be beside the point. In the age of the Internet, it is not hard to imagine critics excitedly claiming, on the authority of anonymous sources, that the former pope privately disapproves of this or that among his successor's decisions.

Italian Church observer Sandro Magister reported on the writing of Church historian Roberto de Mattei, a traditionalist Catholic leader in Italy. On his website *Corrispondenza Romana*, de Mattei did not contest the legitimacy of Benedict XVI's renunciation of the pontificate as he recognized that "it is contemplated by canon law and has been seen historically over the centuries." But he argued that it "appears to be in absolute discontinuity with the tradition and praxis of the Church":

One cannot make a comparison either with Celestine V, who quit after being dragged away by force from his hermit's cell, or with Gregory XII, who was forced to resign in order to resolve the very serious question of the Great Western Schism. These were exceptional cases. But what is the exception in the action of Benedict XVI? . . .

Physical well-being has never been a criterion of governance of the Church. Will it be so beginning with Benedict XVI? The image of the pontifical institution, in the eyes of public opinion all over the world, would in fact be stripped of its sacrality to be handed over to the criteria of judgment of modernity.

Secular Reaction

The secular media, predictably, used the resignation as an occasion to call upon the Church to renounce her teachings on a long laundry list of issues that have been discussed for decades: an end to the Church's opposition to abortion, contraception, so-called same-sex marriage, the ordination of women, and priestly celibacy.

Further, the Church was seen as a corporation in dire need of re-branding and better marketing. On the day of the announcement, for example, ABC's "World News" anchor Diane Sawyer confronted Cardinal Timothy Dolan of New York about the purported need for change. "What would you like to see this next pope be and do in order to be as inclusive as possible of the American Church and the American views on these social issues?" She added, "There has to be fundamental change." Unsurprisingly, Dolan disagreed with her premise.

A study by the Culture and Media Institute focused on the language used by the American television media over the days between the announcement of Benedict's resignation and his departure from the Apostolic Palace on February 28. The word choices revealed a deep-seated bias: the phrase "troubled Church" was used 122 times in 112 stories; "scandal" was used 87 times; the call to "modernize" was used 32 times; and demands that the Church change her teachings on gay marriage were made 13 times.

Nevertheless, the vast majority of U.S. Catholics gave Pope Benedict XVI high marks for his handling of the papacy. According to a survey by Pew Research Center released on February 22, 74 percent of U.S. Catholics "express a favorable view of the pope." The rating was similar to that of March 2008, when about three in four Catholics held a "very" or "mostly" favorable opinion of the pope shortly before his visit to the United States. Pope Benedict had also been regarded favorably throughout his entire papacy, with approval ratings among U.S. Catholics ranging from 67 to 83 percent.

The level of the pope's popularity remained a surprise to the media that was once again shocked to report on the immense crowd of more than one hundred and fifty thousand people who attended Benedict XVI's second-to-last Angelus in St. Peter's Square. The pope used the occasion to focus on Lent as "a time of conversion and penitence in preparation for Easter."

He said:

In this Year of Faith, Lent is a favorable time to rediscover faith in God as the fundamental criterion of our lives and the life of the Church. This always implies a struggle, spiritual combat, because the spirit of evil, naturally, opposes our sanctification and tries to turn us from God's path. . . .

The tempter is sly: he doesn't push us directly toward evil, but toward a false good, making us believe that power and that which satisfies our basic needs are the true realities. In this way, God becomes secondary; he is reduced to a means, becomes unreal, no longer counts, disappears. In the final analysis, faith is what is at stake in temptation because God is at stake.

In the decisive moments of our lives, but on closer inspection in every moment, we are faced with a choice: do we want to follow the "I" or God? Do we want to seek out selfish interests or the true Good. . . ?

The Lenten Exercises

Focus next turned to the long-planned Lenten Spiritual Exercises of the Holy Father that are traditionally held for the papal household and most of the Roman Curia. The exercises were held February 17-23 in the Redemptoris Mater chapel in the Apostolic Palace.

Attention was especially high on the part of Vatican observers because of who was presenting the daily meditations. By prearrangement, Pope Benedict had asked Cardinal Gianfranco Ravasi, president of the Pontifical Council for Culture, to deliver the reflections. Ravasi was considered a possible candidate to the papacy as Benedict's successor. As the previous meditations had been delivered by other prominent *papabili*, including the 1976 spiritual exercises delivered by then Cardinal Karol Wojtyla of Kraków, who was elected to the papacy two years later, there was intense scrutiny of the words of Cardinal Ravasi.

Ravasi's meditations led off by depicting Pope Benedict's future role in the Church as similar to that of Moses who went onto the mountain to pray for the people of Israel. In subsequent reflections, Ravasi focused on the phenomenon of human sinfulness, noting God's work of reconciliation. He stressed the drama of the human person without God, saying that this absence can be "felt painfully and disturbingly, even by believers." He added, "Faith includes absence, silence, bewilderment."

"Absence is not God's last word," however. The cardinal pointed to Psalm 22, which concludes with the salvific response of God himself to the cries of his servant who praises his Savior, who, "has not despised or abhorred the affliction of the afflicted; and he has not hid his face from him, but has heard, when he cried to him" (v. 24).

The meditations proved to be a powerful start to the events of the last week of Benedict's pontificate. Those final days, however, were marked by a firestorm of controversy that seemed at times poised to engulf the very conclave seeking to find a worthy successor.

The Media Maelstrom

Even as the Spiritual Exercises were starting at the Apostolic Palace, the media continued apace with its own efforts to dissect the story and shape it. On February 17, *The New York Times* offered a breathless question in its Vatican City Memo — "When a Pope Retires, Is He Still Infallible?" — in which Rachel Donadio observed: "In transforming an office with an aura of divinity into something far more human, Benedict's decision has sent shock waves through the Vatican hierarchy, who next month will elect his successor. But it has also puzzled the faithful and scholars, who wonder how a pope can be infallible one day and fallible again the next — and whether that might undermine the authority of church teaching."

Only in one small paragraph does she answer the issue with the official Vatican response — namely, "The Vatican spokesman, the Rev. Federico Lombardi, has repeatedly said that Canon Law ensures the infallibility of Benedict's successor, and that once he retires, Benedict will no longer have the authority to promulgate dogma."

Four days later, the center-left-leaning newspaper *La Repubblica* of Rome splashed across its front page a vague, unsourced story that was quickly picked up by the world's major news agencies. In essence the story said that the investigation commissioned by Pope Benedict into the theft of his papers (the so-called Vatileaks scandal) had led, supposedly, to a tawdry revelation of high-ranking Vatican officials caught up in a gay cabal of blackmail and financial misdeeds. What made the story especially tempting for the media was its claim that the pope had made the decision to resign on December 17, the day he received the Vatileaks report from the three cardinals who conducted the investigation. But as we have already seen, the decision to resign had been made many months before.

Longtime Vatican watcher John Allen, writing about the story in the February 22 edition of the *National Catholic Reporter*, pointed to the accountability already on the agenda for many:

> Among many cardinals, it's become a fixed point of faith that the Vatican is long overdue for a serious housecleaning, and certainly the furor unleashed by the *La Repubblica* piece is likely to strengthen that conviction.

Adding to the tumult a few days later, Cardinal Keith O'Brien, archbishop of Saint Andrews and Edinburgh, in Scotland, was accused of inappropriate sexual conduct in a series of well-timed anonymous allegations. Pope Benedict immediately accepted his resignation, and the archbishop decided not to attend the upcoming conclave.

The Vatican Responds

For its part, the Vatican responded to the *La Repubblica* story on February 21 with a forceful denunciation. Framed within the context of the wider conclave that was about to be convoked and the threat being posed to the deliberations of the cardinals, the response had broad application:

> The freedom of the College of Cardinals, which, by law, is responsible for providing for the election of the Roman Pontiff, has always been strongly defended by the Holy See as the guarantee of a choice based solely on deliberations directed toward the good of the Church.
>
> Over the course of the centuries, cardinals have had to face many forms of pressures, exerted upon individual electors or upon the College of Cardinals itself, that sought to influence their decisions, following a political or worldly logic.
>
> If in the past the so-called powers, i.e., States, sought to influence the election of the pope, today there is an attempt to do this through public opinion, which is often based on judgments that do not capture the typically spiritual aspect of this moment that the Church is living.
>
> It is deplorable that, as we draw closer to the moment that the conclave will begin and the cardinal electors will be held — in conscience and before God — to freely express their choice, there is a widespread distribution of often unverified, unverifiable, or even completely false news stories that cause serious damage to persons and institutions.
>
> Never before as at this moment are Catholics focusing on what is essential: praying for Pope Benedict, praying that the Holy Spirit might enlighten the College of Cardinals, and praying for the future pope, confident that the future of the barque of Peter is in God's hands.

The Pope's Last Audience

By the start of the final week of Pope Benedict's pontificate, attention at last returned to where it needed to be: on the Holy Father and the last days of his time on the throne of Peter. The days proved intensely emotional, starting with his last Angelus address on Sunday, February 24. The Gospel that day focused on the Transfiguration of the Lord (see Lk 9:28-36). More than 150,000 people packed into St. Peter's Square for the event, and the pope took as his theme the fact that in Luke's Gospel Jesus was transfigured as he prayed:

His is a profound experience of relationship with the Father during a sort of spiritual retreat . . . in the company of Peter, James, and John, the three disciples always present in moments of divine manifestation of the Master. . . .

Peter's words: "Master, it is good that we are here" (9:33) represents the impossible attempt to stop this mystical experience. St. Augustine says: "[Peter] . . . on the mountain . . . had Christ as the food of the soul. Why should he come down to return to the labors and pains, while up there he was full of feelings of holy love for God that inspired in him a holy conduct?" (Sermon 78.3)

We can draw a very important lesson from meditating on this passage of the Gospel. First, the primacy of prayer, without which all the work of the apostolate and of charity is reduced to activism. In Lent we learn to give proper time to prayer, both personal and communal, which gives breath to our spiritual life. In addition, to pray is not to isolate oneself from the world and its contradictions, as Peter wanted on Tabor, instead prayer leads us back to the path, to action.

The Christian life — I wrote in my Message for Lent — consists in continuously scaling the mountain to meet God and then coming back down, bearing the love and strength drawn from him, so as to serve our brothers and sisters with God's own love.

The pope finished with a personal reflection:

Dear brothers and sisters, I feel that this Word of God is particularly directed at me, at this point in my life. The Lord is calling me to "climb the mountain," to devote myself even more to prayer and meditation. But this does not mean abandoning the Church, indeed, if God is asking me to do this it is so that I can continue to serve the Church with the same dedication and the same love with which I have done thus far, but in a way that is better suited to my age and my strength. Let us invoke the intercession of the Virgin Mary: may she always help us all to follow the Lord Jesus in prayer and works of charity.

It was a powerful moment, and a return to his most basic purpose in resigning. As he declared, he was not giving up or abandoning the Church. He would continue to serve, but in a different way, through

---

☩

---

*The Lord is calling me to "climb the mountain," to devote myself
even more to prayer and meditation. But this does not mean abandoning the Church.*

— POPE BENEDICT XVI

---

prayer and meditation. He would serve in a way that was best suited
for his strength and energies, but he would still serve.

Literally thousands of journalists had gathered in Rome by Monday. The networks painted pictures of gloom and near despair surrounding the Vatican, but the atmosphere in St. Peter's Square starting
Tuesday was remarkably upbeat, though tear-filled.

On Wednesday, February 27, a bright clear but chilly day dawned,
and the throng that had started assembling the day before began filling the square. By the start of the audience there were more than
200,000 in attendance. Many carried banners and signs thanking
Pope Benedict for his love of the Church and giving assurance of their
prayerful support. It was an emotional moment as the pontiff rode for
the last time in the popemobile and circled the crowds, even stopping
to kiss a baby on the way.

He said, in part:

> Thank you for coming in such large numbers to this last General
> Audience of my pontificate. . . .
>
> At this time, I have within myself a great trust [in God],
> because I know — all of us know — that the Gospel's word of
> truth is the strength of the Church: it is her life. The Gospel
> purifies and renews: it bears fruit wherever the community of
> believers hears and welcomes the grace of God in truth and lives
> in charity. This is my faith; this is my joy.
>
> When, almost eight years ago, on April 19 [2005], I agreed to
> take on the Petrine ministry, I held steadfast in this certainty,
> which has always accompanied me. In that moment, as I have
> already stated several times, the words that resounded in my
> heart were: "Lord, what do you ask of me? It is a great weight that
> You place on my shoulders, but, if You ask me, at your word I

will throw out the nets, sure that you will guide me" — and the Lord really has guided me. He has been close to me: daily could I feel His presence.

[These years] have been a stretch of the Church's pilgrim way, which has seen moments of joy and light, but also difficult moments. I have felt like Saint Peter with the Apostles in the boat on the Sea of Galilee: the Lord has given us many days of sunshine and gentle breeze, days in which the catch has been abundant; [then] there have been times when the seas were rough and the wind against us, as in the whole history of the Church it has ever been — and the Lord seemed to sleep.

Nevertheless, I always knew that the Lord is in the barque, that the barque of the Church is not mine, not ours, but his — and he shall not let her sink. It is he who steers her: to be sure, he does so also through men of his choosing, for he desired that it be so. This was and is a certainty that nothing can tarnish. It is for this reason that today my heart is filled with gratitude to God, for never did he leave me or the Church without his consolation, his light, his love.

We are in the Year of Faith, which I desired in order to strengthen our own faith in God in a context that seems to push faith more and more toward the margins of life. I would like to invite everyone to renew firm trust in the Lord. I would like that we all entrust ourselves as children to the arms of God, and rest assured that those arms support us and help us to walk every day, even in times of struggle. I would like everyone to feel loved by the God who gave his Son for us and showed us his boundless love. I want everyone to feel the joy of being Christian.

A beautiful prayer to be recited daily in the morning says: "I adore you, my God, I love you with all my heart. I thank You for having created me, for having made me a Christian." Yes, we are happy for the gift of faith: it is the most precious good, that no one can take from us! Let us thank God for this every day, with prayer and with a coherent Christian life. God loves us, but he also expects that we love him!

Pope Benedict then went on to thank all those who had supported him in his ministry, from the cardinals to people throughout the world who sent "tokens of concern, friendship, and prayer."

I . . . receive many letters from ordinary people who write to me simply from their heart and let me feel their affection, which is born of our being together in Christ Jesus, in the Church. These people do not write me as one might write, for example, to a prince or a great figure one does not know. They write as brothers and sisters, sons and daughters, with the sense of very affectionate family ties. Here, one can touch what the Church is — not an organization, not an association for religious or humanitarian purposes, but a living body, a community of brothers and sisters in the Body of Jesus Christ, who unites us all. To experience the Church in this way and almost be able to touch with one's hands the power of his truth and his love, is a source of joy, in a time in which many speak of its decline.

In recent months, I felt that my strength had decreased, and I asked God with insistence in prayer to enlighten me with his light to make me take the right decision — not for my sake, but for the good of the Church. I have taken this step in full awareness of its severity and also its novelty, but with a deep peace of mind. Loving the Church also means having the courage to make difficult, trying choices, having ever before oneself the good of the Church and not one's own.

Here allow me to return once again to April 19, 2005. The gravity of the decision was precisely in the fact that from that moment on I was committed always and forever by the Lord. Always — he, who assumes the Petrine ministry no longer has any privacy. He belongs always and totally to everyone, to the whole Church. His life is, so to speak, totally deprived of the private sphere. I have felt, and I feel even in this very moment, that one receives one's life precisely when he offers it as a gift. . . .

The "always" is also a "forever" — there is no returning to private life. My decision to forgo the exercise of active ministry does not revoke this. I do not return to private life, to a life of travel, meetings, receptions, conferences, and so on. I do not abandon the Cross, but remain in a new way near to the Crucified Lord. I no longer wield the power of the office for the government of the Church, but in the service of prayer I remain, so to speak, within Saint Peter's bounds. Saint Benedict, whose name I bear as pope, shall be a great example in this for me. He showed us the way to a life which, active or passive, belongs wholly to the work of God.

I thank each and every one of you for the respect and understanding with which you have welcomed this important decision. . . . I ask you to remember me before God, and above all to pray for the cardinals, who are called to so important a task, and for the new Successor of Peter, that the Lord might accompany him with the light and the power of his Spirit.

Let us invoke the maternal intercession of Mary, Mother of God and of the Church, that she might accompany each of us and the whole ecclesial community: to her we entrust ourselves, with deep trust.

Dear friends! God guides his Church, maintains her always, and especially in difficult times. Let us never lose this vision of faith, which is the only true vision of the way of the Church and the world. In our heart, in the heart of each of you, let there be always the joyous certainty that the Lord is near, that he does not abandon us, that he is near to us, and that he surrounds us with his love. Thank you!

In attendance also were the members of the College of Cardinals who had reached Rome in anticipation of the papal resignation. Tears streamed down the faces of some of the members as they were overcome by emotion at the farewell. Weeping and cheers of *"Viva il Papa!"* filled the square as well.

And then, the popemobile retired back into the Apostolic Palace. The last audience was over, and the final evening of the pontificate was marked by a perfectly clear sky, a bright shining moon rising behind the lit dome of Saint Peter's Basilica.

The Last Day

February 28, like the day before, dawned bright and crisp in Rome. Crowds continued to form outside the papal palace and Saint Peter's, not in the hope of glimpsing the pope one last time but to witness history, to pray for the pontiff, and to express publicly one last time the gratitude of the Church's faithful for his life of service.

Within the Apostolic Palace, it was a day that witnessed events unseen in the long history of the Vatican. When Celestine V had reigned, he had done so in a different world. The pope in 1294 had renounced the papacy, but he had been in Naples, not Rome. And until the end of the fourteenth century and the return of the papacy from Avignon, France, the popes of the era did not reside in the Vatican regularly; they lived in the Lateran Palace across the Tiber from Vatican Hill. When Gregory XII resigned in 1415, he had done so in the city of Rimini.

The departure of Benedict XVI, then, was an event that not even the Vatican had ever seen. It was, indeed, something entirely new.

As had been previously announced, the members of the College of Cardinals who were in Rome and were able to attend gathered in the Clementine Hall in the Apostolic Palace to say farewell to their pontiff. The pope greeted each of the 144 cardinals individually, together with the presidents and officials of the different Vatican offices, and delivered a final address saying, among other things:

> I would like to leave you with a simple thought that is close to my heart, a thought on the Church, her mystery, which is for all of us, we can say, the reason and the passion of our lives. I am helped by an expression of Romano Guardini's, written in the year in which the fathers of the Second Vatican Council approved the constitution *Lumen Gentium*. . . .
>
> Guardini says: "The Church is not an institution devised and built at table, but a living reality. She lives along the course of time by transforming herself, like any living being, yet her nature remains the same. At her heart is Christ."
>
> This was our experience yesterday, I think, in the square. We could see that the Church is a living body, animated by the Holy Spirit, and truly lives by the power of God, She is in the world but not of the world. She is of God, of Christ, of the Spirit, as we saw yesterday. This is why another eloquent expression of Guardini's is also true: "The Church is awakening in souls."
>
> The Church lives, grows, and awakens in those souls, which like the Virgin Mary, accept and conceive the Word of God by the power of the Holy Spirit. They offer to God their flesh and in their own poverty and humility become capable of giving birth to Christ in the world today. Through the Church the mystery of the Incarnation remains present forever. Christ continues to walk through all times in all places. . . .

Prior to bidding farewell to each of you personally, I want to tell you that I will continue to be close to you in prayer, especially in the next few days, so that you may all be fully docile to the action of the Holy Spirit in the election of the new pope. May the Lord show you what is willed by him. And among you, among the College of Cardinals, there is also the future pope, to whom, here today, I already promise my unconditional reverence and obedience. For all this, with affection and gratitude, I cordially impart upon you my Apostolic Blessing.

The crowds only grew in size in Saint Peter's Square, and the large television screens that were used to carry images of Pope Benedict's Masses and liturgies now revealed the final moments of his pontificate. Vatican Television broadcast to an eager world the last journey of Benedict through the Apostolic Palace as he bid farewell to the Gentlemen-of-His-Holiness, the staff of the Secretariat of State, and the many caretakers of the home of the popes. With his cane in hand, he made his way through the magnificent corridors of the palace until he came at last to the waiting automobile that took him into the recesses of the Vatican Gardens. There, at the highest part of the verdant papal retreat, he reached the helipad and the helicopter that was ready to take him from the Vatican City State.

As the crowds scanned the skyline or watched the television screens in Saint Peter's Square, the helicopter lifted off around 4:45 p.m. and made its way over the dome of the basilica and then across the Eternal City toward the Alban Hills to the west. The bells of Saint Peter's began to toll in a final salute, reminding the world that nearly eight years before they had rung out to announce the swift election of this same pontiff. When they fell silent after a time few in the crowd realized that they would ring one last time for Benedict, at 8:00 p.m., to announce the official end of his pontificate. Millions watched around the world. In the square, thousands prayed, others waved farewell, many cried.

Around 5:20 p.m., the pope reached the summer residence of Castel Gandolfo. There another large crowd filled the Piazza della Libertà beneath the window of the palace. To the great joy of the faithful, the pontiff came to the balcony and addressed them:

Thank you . . . [for] your friendship that does me so much good, thank you for your friendship, for caring.

You know that today is different from others . . . as of 8:00 p.m. I will no longer be the Supreme Pontiff of the Catholic Church. I will simply be a pilgrim who is beginning the last part of his pilgrimage on earth.

But with my heart, my love, my prayer, with all my inner strength, I will work for the common good and the good of the Church and all humanity.

And I feel greatly supported by your affection. Let us move forward together with the Lord for the good of the Church and the world.

I will now impart upon you all my Apostolic Blessing.

Thank you and good night. Thank you all.

The pontiff then walked back into the palace. It was his last public appearance as pope. The crowds still waited, though, waiting to see what would happen, some out of curiosity, others still with a sense of disbelief.

At the striking of the bell, at the appointed time, the squad of the Swiss Guard closed the massive wooden doors of the palace at Castel Gandolfo and officially departed the service of Benedict XVI. At that moment, the resignation of Pope Benedict came into effect. The Swiss Guard — charged with protecting the Supreme Pontiff — was now without a pope to protect, and the security of the pope emeritus passed to the Vatican gendarmes.

With the closing of the doors of the palace at Castel Gandolfo at precisely 8:00 p.m., the pontificate of Pope Benedict XVI had ended. Benedict soon presented the Ring of the Fisherman to be defaced by the Cardinal camerlengo, Tarcisio Bertone, and the photograph soon circulated worldwide of Bertone sealing the papal apartments. The doors would not be opened again until the arrival of the new pope in some weeks' time.

The Church had entered into the time of the *sede vacante*.

Chapter Three

"YOU LOOK FOR A MAN WHO REMINDS YOU OF JESUS"

—✠—

"I mean it when you say you look for a man who reminds you of Jesus. When we see [the pope], we're immediately elevated to the things beyond, the eternal truth and to the man who described himself as the truth, Jesus Christ."

— CARDINAL TIMOTHY DOLAN,
ARCHBISHOP OF NEW YORK, ON CNN

March 1 dawned to the start of the first full day of the *sede vacante* in Rome and for the entire Church. The traditional symbol of the interregnum — the crossed keys beneath the umbrella, the symbol of the camerlengo who manages administrative business in the interim — was now the order of the day. Reporters and pilgrims in the Eternal City began snatching up the first available sets of coins and stamps from the Vatican Numismatic and Philatelic Office that marked the event.

The Cardinals Begin Their Work

Over the next few days, some of the larger media outlets sent a number of their correspondents home, with the plan for them to return to the Eternal City once the date for the conclave was set. Nevertheless, that still left a huge contingent of the world's press, and the numbers ticked slowly up again as the conclave drew closer. By the end of the first week in March there were 4,432 temporarily accredited journalists and 600 permanently accredited journalists from 1,004 news outlets, 65 nations, and representing 24 languages.

The Vatican's Sala Stampa, or Press Office, was working hard to satisfy the endless media requests. Given the overwhelming number of journalists on hand, the office served some from its facilities on the Via della Conciliazione but moved the overflow to the Synod Hall on the grounds of the Vatican.

Meanwhile, the world's news organizations claimed the rooftops of the buildings surrounding Saint Peter's Basilica, all jostling to have an unobstructed view of the basilica and St. Peter's Square for the days to come.

The North American College, the seminary for Americans study-ing in Rome that is perched on the Janiculum Hill, became a kind of ground zero for reporters as they tracked down cardinals in hopes of securing interviews. Most of the American cardinals who had come from the United States for the conclave took up residence at the semi-nary — many were alumni, including Cardinal Dolan who had been rector there from 1994 to 2001 — and they were remarkably available to reporters. They spoke at times candidly about what they wanted to see happen in the general congregations (meetings before the con-clave), and to some degree what they were searching for in candi-dates for the papacy. They were patient with the sometimes irritating questions from American reporters about the need for the Church to "reform," and their interviews played out on every network and appeared in multiple newspapers and online.

The interviews with the Americans and the other cardinals were parsed and examined for hints about the upcoming vote, often in almost comical ways, but the optics were obvious: the cardinals had started going about their work to find the next Successor to Peter.

To be sure, the preceding days of the resignation and then the emotional departure of Pope Benedict XVI had been virtually unprec-edented in the life of modern Catholicism, but the mechanisms of law, tradition, and protocol were now triggered. What this meant in practical terms was that while it was true that the Church had an offi-cially titled "pope emeritus" for the first time, and the first resigned pope in 600 years, the process for choosing his successor would now proceed. It would do so along the lines clearly enunciated in Church law, especially the papal election decree of *Universi Dominici Gregis* of Pope Blessed John Paul II, with its minor but not insignificant revi-sions by Pope Benedict XVI.

The resignation of Pope Benedict had established the major context for the conclave to elect a new Supreme Pontiff. But in the days that followed the start of the *sede vacante*, the resignation itself became one of the issues — but not the only one — with which the cardinals grappled as they prepared to enter the Sistine Chapel. As Cardinal John Onaiyekan of Abuja, Nigeria, said to John Allen in an interview for the *National Catholic Reporter*: "You know, when you go to a Synod of Bishops for the first time, you look for those who have been there before. But this time, even the over-80 cardinals are saying there's something special about this *sede vacante*. It means there's something new. As a result, nobody really knows what to do. No one has gone through this kind of thing before, and it's come up more than once that we need time to really discern what exactly it means to have a conclave with a living pope."

The *Motu Proprio*

The immediate question — when would the conclave begin? — drove home just how unusual the situation was. The pope had not died, so the tradition of the *novemdiales*, or nine days of Masses and mourning, did not take effect, and it caused some to wonder if it was still necessary or even desirable for the cardinals to wait the minimum of fifteen days after the start of the *sede vacante* before convening the conclave.

The answer was that the laws governing the conclave had been set largely by John Paul II and remained in force. The terms were unambiguous. The cardinals were not empowered to make changes in law, either while there was still a pontiff leading the Church or once the interregnum had begun. Within days of the announced resignation, then, the assumption had been that Benedict would make some amendment to the laws governing the *sede vacante*.

On February 22, Benedict issued a *motu proprio*, or apostolic document on his own initiative, titled *Normas Nonnullas*, in which he made certain modifications to the laws for the *sede vacante*. Aside from reminding the cardinals of the importance of secrecy, going so far as to demand an oath from everyone involved, and imposing excommunication upon violators, the pope gave the College of Cardinals permission to move the start date.

THE CARDINAL ELECTORS

The College of Cardinals as of March 12 was comprised of 207 members from 67 countries, but only those under the age of 80 years were eligible to vote in a conclave. There were 117 cardinal electors from 50 countries; however, only 115 cardinals actually entered the Sistine Chapel. Cardinal Julius Darmaatmadja of Indonesia did not travel owing to reasons of health, and Cardinal Keith O'Brien of Scotland retired from public life owing to sexual impropriety. Pope John Paul II had named fifty of the cardinal electors, and Pope Benedict XVI had appointed sixty-seven.

Geographical Distribution
Europe: 61 cardinals from 18 countries
North America: 17 cardinals from 14 countries
South America: 16 cardinals from 11 countries
Africa: 11 cardinals from 8 countries
Asia: 11 cardinals from 7 countries
Oceania: 1 cardinal from 1 country

Countries with the Most Electors
Italy: 28
United States: 11
Germany: 6
Brazil: 5
India: 5
Spain: 5
France: 4
Poland: 4
Canada: 3
México: 3

Oldest cardinal elector: Cardinal Walter Kasper, who turned 80 on March 5, but was still eligible to vote because the *sede vacante* began on February 28.

Youngest cardinal elector: Cardinal Baselios Cleemis Thottunkal, 53.

Average age of cardinal electors: 72.

The General Congregations

On March 1, 2013, Cardinal Angelo Sodano, the 85-year-old Dean of the College of Cardinals and former Secretary of State under Pope John Paul II, sent out the formal letter to the world's cardinals summoning them officially to Rome. He stated that Pope Benedict XVI had resigned the papacy as of February 28, at 8:00 p.m., and that the terms of the papal election decree were now in force. He then called on them to make their way to the Paul VI Audience Hall in the Vatican, specifically the *sala* (office) of the Synod of Bishops on Monday, March 4, 9:30 a.m., for the first of the general congregations.

The general congregations are the most important pre-conclave gatherings for the cardinals, all of whom take part, even those over the age of 80 who will not be voting in the conclave. The meetings review the laws that govern the voting, set a date for the start of the conclave, and begin the vital process of discussing the key issues facing the Church at the present time.

The congregations also offer the cardinals the opportunity to get to know each other better and to see each other in action as they consider who among them is the most qualified to be successor to Saint Peter. Cardinal Francis George told reporters during one of the press conferences at the North American College: "I would imagine each of us has some kind of a list of primary candidates and other secondary and tertiary. There's a likely list at this point — it isn't winnowed yet — of people who might be considered candidates."

Meanwhile, the press and the tens of thousands of pilgrims who had come to the Eternal City for the conclave often saw the cardinals — both the electors and those over the age of 80 — around Rome. Roman cab drivers, typically well-informed of the goings-on of the cardinals, offered their free opinions as to which cardinal was rising or falling, relying on snippets of conversations they might have picked up during a fare. For their part, the cardinals did not spend a great deal of time in public places such as restaurants, intent on keeping their conversations discreet.

The press, not surprisingly, focused less on the collegial atmosphere of the general congregations and more on the supposed politicking and alliance building. In this regard, the interregnum proved unusually filled with reports of intrigue and plotting, with the main theme being that the Vatican old guard was eager for a swift start to the conclave while cardinals from around the world wanted a delay to get a better sense of the reformer candidates.

Arguably, the most curious report in the Italian papers came from *La Repubblica* on March 2 stating that a group of cardinals favored the election of a cardinal over the age of 80 who would have the sole task of reforming the Curia. This would mean, of course, electing someone not even eligible to vote in the conclave. The notion didn't seem to find any traction among cardinals who were asked about it.

Noted Vaticanista Andrea Tornielli and reporter Gerard O'Connell proposed another theory in the "Vatican Insider" section of the online edition of the Italian newspaper *La Stampa*. They wrote: "Sources both within and outside the Vatican confirm that a new group in the Vatican are [sic] seeking to bring for the first time in history a Latin American to the See of Peter, accompanied by a Secretary of State who is Italian, or an Argentinian of Italian origins. Among the proponents of this initiative are two leading cardinals — Angelo Sodano, the Dean of the College of Cardinals, and Giovanni Battista Re. Other important Italian curial cardinals could join this initiative." This group's candidate to be pope "is the Archbishop of São Paolo, Brazil, Odilo Pedro Scherer, 63 . . ."

While many experts in Rome soon dismissed all of the proposed schemes, it made for intense reading. But it also gave the false and unseemly appearance that some cardinals had reduced the profound duty of finding the next Vicar of Christ to nothing but a political campaign or an intrigue-filled game of power and self-serving ambitions.

Despite these caricatures, the cardinals tried to remain as attentive as possible to the needs of the world's media. That ended suddenly on March 6 with the collective decision that there would be no further press access to individual cardinals. Sister Mary Ann Walsh, the hard-working media relations director for the United States Conference of Catholic Bishops, who had moved with much of her staff to Rome for the duration of the conclave, sent out an e-mail explaining why silence had descended on the College of Cardinals: "Due to concerns over accounts being reported in the Italian press, which breached confidentiality, the College of Cardinals has agreed not to give interviews."

There was grumbling among the reporters that the cardinals had been gagged. Longtime Vatican reporter John Thavis blogged, "In other words, because some anonymous cardinals fed Italian reporters a few details about their discussions, a gag order now applies to all the cardinals." And there was open complaint that the real reason for the decision was the unhappiness of some in the Vatican establishment with the openness of the American cardinals and the popularity of their press conferences at the North American College. The Americans were not divulging secrets of the general congregations, but were providing insights to the press about the critical issues facing the Church. It had been a great exercise in effective application of Catholic social communications.

The Conclave's Issues

When not in their general congregations, the cardinals were meeting and talking together quietly — in the residences of the cardinals in Rome and in the many national seminaries across the city. Both law and custom forbid active campaigning by a cardinal, but discussions sought to bring into harmony a triad of concerns: the will of the Holy Spirit, the state of the Church, and finding the right person who would be able to meet the demands imposed on him and prove truly worthy to follow Benedict. Such small get-togethers had always been crucial in setting the direction for a subsequent conclave, because it was there, in the quiet of conversation, that personalities could be discerned, reflections on ecclesiastical matters revealed, and genuine friendships established between prelates who might only have met a few times in previous consistories or irregular travel and symposia.

Cardinal George told reporters that aside from the general congregations, the private conversations were where the cardinals assessed candidates and asked questions of one another, such as, "What do you know about this candidate? And could you tell me how he would react to this? And what sort of person is he, what's his personality?" Cardinal Wilfrid Napier of Durban, South Africa, said in an interview with Catholic News Service that he thought the cardinals were "closer" to each other in 2013 than in 2005, although he admitted that he still needed to Google some of his fellow cardinals to find out more about them.

Only fifty of the 115 had taken part in the previous conclave in 2005, and there were twenty-four new members just since 2012. As Cardinal Thomas Collins of Toronto said in an interview with Vatican Radio, "I think one of our chief responsibilities is to be very conscious of the needs of the universal Church and also to get to know the other cardinals; we don't always have an opportunity to do that, and so these days before the conclave but after the see is vacant is a tremendous opportunity for all the cardinals to discuss the issues with one another, to get to know one another better, and therefore to be better prepared for the moment when those who are cardinal electors enter into the conclave."

Pope Benedict XVI arrived at the papacy not only as the oldest pontiff in 300 years, but as the inheritor of the enormous body of teachings and the experiences of the pontificate of John Paul II. He was thus positioned to carry forward that legacy and to make his own contributions to the rich treasury of papal teachings. Aware of the limited energies he brought to bear, however, he chose his priorities. One of those was to continue the work of implementing the authentic teachings of the Second Vatican Council, striving for a genuine renewal and reform of the Church, particularly in the areas of the liturgy, the priesthood, and Catholic identity. He had focused especially on bringing an end to the sex abuse crisis, on the relationship between faith and reason, and on the New Evangelization.

As with the pontificate of Pope John Paul II — ultimately with every pontificate — there was a sense with Benedict of unfinished business. The needs of the Church, of course, are conditioned by exquisitely precise historical circumstances. This seemed even more the case because of the papal resignation. The cardinals were not openly critical of the pontiff, but they could enumerate areas where work remained to be done.

One of the tasks at hand for the cardinals, then, was delineating the main issues for the Church at this moment in time. In both the general congregations and the media encounters, the cardinals seemed to focus heavily on four topics:

- Reform of the Curia
- Sex Abuse Crisis
- The Needs of the Global Church
- The New Evangelization

Reform of the Curia

Over the course of the final years of Benedict's pontificate, it had seemed at times that the entire Vatican was habitually battered by scandals, infighting, and even incompetence.

Even as the Western media repeated inaccurate and misleading accusations that the pontiff had failed to deal with the sex abuse crisis or had even supposedly greenlighted coverups involving abusive priests (a story thoroughly proven to be false), fresh scandals were reported relating to severe ineptitude or even worse in Vatican finances, especially at the Vatican Bank, called the IOR (*l'Istituto per le Opere di Religione*), or the Institute for Works of Religion.

The Vatican Bank had long been the subject of scrutiny and conspiracy theories, but the oversight of cardinals from around the world had helped to clean up the system. It was consequently a depressing step backward in December 2010 when the tough Roman financial police found severe failings in the way the bank was operating, and then Italian magistrates froze 23 million euros (approximately $33 million) that IOR held in an Italian bank. The funds were subsequently released in June 2011, but investigations continued, and another embarrassment came in July 2012 when Moneyval, a monitoring committee of the 47-nation Council of Europe, issued a scathing report that said the Vatican Bank had failed to meet its standards and had actually passed only nine of sixteen "key and core" aspects of its financial checklist. For its part, the Vatican pledged full cooperation with the European Union's financial control system, but it was a humiliation and was used by critics to point to the Holy See's apparent inability to modernize its business and financial practices.

In May 2012, just before the Moneyval report, the bank's own internationally composed oversight committee fired the head of the bank, Ettore Gotti Tedeschi. Lost in the reporting on Pope Benedict's resignation was the appointment on February 15, 2013, of Ernst von Freyberg as the new head of the IOR. It was generally agreed that his first order of business was to re-organize the internal administration of the bank, but he also had the task of improving the image of an institution that serves the Church in her global mission.

Unfortunately, by the time of von Freyberg's appointment, the financial aspects of the Vatican's recent crises had long expanded well beyond simple problems of modernization and transparency. In January 2012, the Italian television program *The Untouchables* (*Gli intoccabili*) released on air a series of confidential letters supposedly written by Archbishop Carlo Maria Viganò, then the number two official in the Governorate of the Vatican City State, to Pope Benedict XVI and the Vatican Secretary of State, Cardinal Tarcisio Bertone. The letters claimed that he had encountered opposition from within the Curia and that he hoped to continue fighting the "corruption and dishonesty" in Vatican finances. He implored the pope and Cardinal Bertone to allow him to remain in his post and continue the job he had been given of improving administrative and financial affairs.

The program was followed immediately by the explosive start to what became known as "Vatileaks." The scandal involved the leak of sensitive Vatican documents, including some of the personal papers of Pope Benedict XVI. The papers were actually published in a book by the Italian journalist Gianluigi Nuzzi, *His Holiness: The Secret Papers of Benedict XVI*, released on May 18, 2012. To deal with the problem of stolen and leaked documents, in March 2012 Pope Benedict appointed three retired cardinals, Julián Herranz and Jozef Tomko, both former Vatican officials, and Salvatore De Giorgi, the former archbishop of Palermo, Italy, to investigate.

On May 23, 2012, Paolo Gabriele, the pontiff's personal butler since 2006, was arrested as one of the main figures in the leaks to Nuzzi. A Vatican court convicted him on October 6, but the maximum sentence was reduced to 18 months in an Italian prison. Pope Benedict pardoned him on December 22, 2012.

Five days before his pardon of Gabriele, the pope met with the three cardinals investigating the leaks, and they gave him their completed report. No one had seen the report save for the pope emeritus and the three cardinals themselves, but it became the centerpiece of the incendiary article in *La Repubblica* in February, with its unattributed claims that what had started as a financial scandal and stolen documents had spiraled down into a cesspool of corrupt Vatican lobbies, cabals of gay priests, blackmail, and a crushed and despairing pope.

To no one's surprise, reporters peppered the cardinals gathering in Rome for the conclave with questions about Vatileaks and the report by the three cardinals. While the report was sealed, the three investigators could discuss its contents and findings, and a number of cardinals expressed a desire for more information. During the general congregations, the scandal thus entered into the wider discussion about the functioning of the Roman Curia and the need for a thoroughgoing reform of its offices.

Cardinal Peter Turkson from Ghana, and the president of the Pontifical Council for Justice and Peace, said of the scandals in an interview with John Thavis, who reported on his blog: "Every time this pops up on Italian television, and you have a crook or Mafia member who has kept his money in the Vatican Bank, that brings the Vatican down the drain, too. . . . We need to work on restoration of credibility. And I would put that probably on top of the list for the successor of Benedict. It's so important because now we're talking about [the] New Evangelization, and every pope has consistently talked about witnesses speaking louder than words. The burden is on us to be credible, to be sincere in everything we do."

The Sex Abuse Crisis

Similarly, the sex abuse crisis — unquestionably one of the most contentious, not to mention damaging, situations facing the Church in the last fifty years — was a critical topic during the cardinal's deliberations. The scandal exploded into modern consciousness in 2001 with the avalanche of cases that fell on the Archdiocese of Boston and led to the resignation of its archbishop, Cardinal Bernard Law.

From that time, the Church in the United States and across parts of Europe and elsewhere has been dealing with lawsuits, attacks upon the credibility of Church leaders, and in recent years deliberate efforts to accuse Pope Benedict XVI himself of negligence and even criminal conspiracies to protect child abusers and pedophiles.

In truth, Benedict XVI presided over an extensive and thorough series of reforms, enabling the Church to learn from the disaster and to incorporate those lessons into a cohesive program of ecclesiastical, canonical, and spiritual reform and renewal. Much work remains to be done, a point made by the American cardinals. At their press conferences at the North American College in Rome, they spoke forthrightly about the crisis and saw it as an issue to be dealt with by the next pope.

Cardinal George declared that the crisis has been a "terrible wound on the body of the Church." He added that there are still victims in need of healing, "And the wound, therefore, is deep in their hearts and minds very often; and as long as it's with them it's with all of us, and that will last for a long time. So the next pope has to be very aware of this."

The Needs of the Global Church

The 115 cardinal electors represented 50 countries spanning every continent in a Church that includes one billion souls. What is thus necessarily important to some in the so-called First World is not the most pressing issue for cardinals from across the globe.

Cardinal John Onaiyekan of Nigeria provided a helpful perspective in an interview with the National Catholic Reporter. He said: "We in Nigeria don't know what's happening in the Roman Curia, so I can't say whether it's running well or not. Even the case of the butler, who took papers off the desk of the pope, for me, is not a big deal. There are those who consider the running of the Roman Curia very important, but I'm more interested in how we're able to project the message of Jesus to our people. Not only Catholics, but everybody . . . those are the issues I'm looking at."

Millions live in poverty in the developing world, often viewed as mere human resources, especially by powerful capitalist countries. Horrific diseases — from AIDS to Ebola — prey on the helpless, tens of thousands of children starve to death and die from common illnesses daily, and civil wars and corrupt regimes often oppress these people. As international companies and corporations exploit the land, concern for the proper stewardship of the earth is forgotten in the name of profit.

In effect, the developing world is where the false idols of the West, as Cardinal Luis Tagle of the Philippines calls them, inflict their most fearsome damage. At the Eucharistic Congress in Dublin in 2012, he said:

> Those who worship false gods also dedicate their lives to them. In reality these false gods are self-interests. To keep these false gods, their worshipers sacrifice other people's lives and the earth . . . while preserving themselves and their interests. How many factory workers are being denied the right wages for the god of profit? How many women are being sacrificed to the god of domination? How many children are being sacrificed to the god of lust? How many trees, rivers, hills are being sacrificed to the god of "progress"? How many poor people are being sacrificed to the god of greed? How many defenseless people are being sacrificed to the god of national security?

The numbers themselves tell a striking tale. Populations, including Catholic ones, are shrinking in Western Europe, but there is swift population growth in the developing world, and the Catholic population is keeping pace. Of the Catholic Church's one billion members, over 700 million are in the developing world.

In effect, the future of the Church is in the Southern Hemisphere. The Synod of Bishops on the New Evangelization that was held in Rome in October 2012 emphasized the significance of this. In their Message to the Faithful, the bishops spoke to each region, giving very specific exhortations. Yet the raw statistics of Catholic growth in the developing world do little to provide a picture of the immense vitality of the faith, just as they can do faint justice to the overwhelming challenges faced by the Church in those regions.

The Catholic Church in Latin America entered the new century with a heightened sense of purpose and organization. Still, Latin America suffers from severe poverty, a continuing disparity between rich and poor, and growing crises of secularism and materialism. The Church continues to grapple as well with native religions, such as

Umbanda in Brazil, that pose risks of syncretist tendencies among Catholics, and serious inroads from the Pentecostal Movement. Cardinal Scherer has been especially dedicated in São Paulo to resisting defections from the Church to these sects. One point often raised in favor of a pope from Latin America is precisely the boost he would provide to those engaged in preventing departures and welcoming back those Catholics who return after a dalliance with such groups.

The Synod of Bishops in 2012 wrote in its message to Latin America:

> Now, in the face of many present challenges, first of all poverty and violence, the Church in Latin America and in the Caribbean is encouraged to live in an ongoing state of mission, announcing the Gospel with hope and joy, forming communities of true missionary disciples of Jesus Christ, showing in the commitment of its sons and daughters how the Gospel could be the source of a new, just, and fraternal society. Religious pluralism also tests your churches and requires a renewed proclamation of the Gospel.

In Asia, the Catholic population is less than 3 percent, but the Church is growing exponentially. In 1910 there were barely 13 million Asian Catholics; today there are 130 million. Still, Catholics and other Christians face severe persecutions in predominately Islamic countries, such as Indonesia and Pakistan. In India, Catholics are under constant threat as a tiny minority in a country where the majority of the people are Hindu.

In China, Christianity is growing steadily, but it is still discouraged by the Communist regime that is responsible for the detention of hundreds of priests, religious, and laypeople, and their employment in slave labor. In its efforts to control the Church, the government has also interfered with the pope's appointment of Chinese bishops. As Cardinal George Pell of Sydney observed in an interview with Catholic News Service: "The challenge in China is to increase freedom. Christianity is spreading in China like it did in the pagan Roman Empire."

The synod wrote to the Church in Asia:

> As a small minority in the continent which houses almost two thirds of the world's population, your presence is a fruitful seed

entrusted to the power of the Spirit, which grows in dialogue with the diverse cultures, with the ancient religions, and with the countless poor. Although often outcast by society and in many places also persecuted, the Church of Asia, with its firm faith, is a valuable presence of Christ's Gospel which proclaims justice, life, and harmony.

In Africa, the Church has flourished over the last century and now boasts over 22,000 seminarians and 50,000 women religious. Such are the numbers of vocations among the native clergy that seminaries cannot be built fast enough, classes are staggered for enrollment purposes, and many seminarians are sent to study elsewhere. Even more significantly, African clergy and religious, like their Asian and Latin American counterparts, are being sent to the United States and Europe to serve in parishes and other places for ministry.

In Africa, as in Asia, the Church also deals squarely with the dire crises of the age. The AIDS epidemic, for example, has killed millions, and Church resources are stretched to the breaking point as Catholics care for the victims and their orphans. Likewise, Catholic charitable efforts feed the hungry, educate the young, and labor to bring hope to those who feel they have little or no hope.

The rise of militant elements in Islam poses dangers in Africa as it does in Asia and the Middle East. Missionaries are murdered, Christians are sold into slavery, and Catholics live under severe disabilities imposed by hard-line Islamic governments. In Nigeria, the bishops have spoken out against the imposition of Islamic law in individual states within the country.

None of these obstacles — poverty, corruption, persecution — have halted the success of evangelization. The synod in 2012 wrote to the Church in Africa:

> We look to you Christians, men and women, who live in the countries of Africa, and we express our gratitude for your witness to the Gospel often in difficult circumstances. We exhort you to revive the evangelization that you received in recent times, to build the Church as the family of God, to strengthen the identity of the family, to sustain the commitment of priests and catechists, especially in the small Christian communities. We affirm

the need to develop the encounter between the Gospel and old and new cultures. Great expectation and a strong appeal is addressed to the world of politics and to the governments of the various countries of Africa, so that, in collaboration with all people of good will, basic human rights may be promoted and the continent freed from violence and conflicts which still afflict it.

The relationship between the developed regions and the other continents has not been lost on the cardinals. The two worlds intersect today because of globalization, but all too often the relationship is one of exploitation and the imposition of secularized values. Pope Benedict XVI discussed this in his encyclical *Caritas in Veritate* ("Charity in Truth"), and Cardinal Tagle of the Philippines captured the same spirit when he said during the International Eucharistic Congress in Dublin in 2012:

> We see in our time so much exchange of words happening at high speed and across national boundaries. But, unfortunately, the world is as divided as ever. Why is communion not achieved in spite of the exchange of words? Because Jesus is not the word they share and receive.
>
> When financial wizards talk about ways of manipulating the economy for their own profit, you do not call that communion; that is corruption! When politicians talk to people about grand promises without intending to fulfill them, you do not call that communion; that is cheating! When the powerful "negotiate" among themselves while neglecting the weak, you do not call that communion; that is oppression! When so-called enterprising persons deal with each other on how women and children could be profitable merchandise, you do not call that communion; that is slavery!
>
> When communion consists in Jesus who is the Word of Life, then the common good becomes central. And that is pleasing to God's eyes.

Finally, tied closely to the progress of the Church in both the developed and developing worlds is the issue of world religions, especially Islam. The Muslim faith is a fast-growing presence in the West and a major force in many developing countries of Africa and Asia. In Western Europe and North America, the minaret of the mosque is appearing in greater numbers across cities from Paris to Denver. In Africa and Indonesia, dialogue and understanding are essential to the very survival of small minority communities of Catholics and other Christians.

The encounter and relationship between Christianity and Islam in the Middle East has been a tortured one in recent years. The flight from the Holy Land and the Middle East by Christians is matched only by the departure of the Christians from the region at the end of the Crusades in the thirteenth century. As the Maronite Patriarch of Antioch, Cardinal Béchara Raï, observed in an interview with *La Stampa*:

> The universal Church and the next pope must never forget that Christianity has its origins in the Middle East. And they should keep in mind what is happening to Christian communities in the Middle East. This is a priority that cannot be ignored. . . . A million and a half Christians have fled from post-Saddam Iraq. And at least 60 percent have left Aleppo [Syria]. There is not one Christian left in Homs [Syria]. The Coptic Church in Egypt is still strong. But with the new Sharia-based laws, things are going to get much harder. Then there are the problems in the Holy Land. . . . Cardinals will also need to take this into consideration during the conclave. If we only discuss the Church's internal problems we risk being one-track minded.

The New Evangelization

The greatest enterprise of Pope Benedict XVI's pontificate was the New Evangelization — essentially, the re-proposing of the Gospel to those who are weak in or have left the Faith and the proclamation of the Gospel to the world. The topic is familiar to the cardinal electors, especially because 50 of the 115 had participated in the Synod of Bishops on the New Evangelization held in Rome in October 2012.

The forces of relativism, materialism, and secularism have generally enjoyed a free hand in the West for many decades, and the results are visible everywhere in the degradation of the culture and the widespread loss of faith, even beyond Europe and North America. Cardinal Oscar Andrés Rodríguez Maradiaga, the archbishop of Tegucigalpa, Honduras, speaking of Latin America on Vatican Radio, said that even there, "God has been displaced by materialism, and the

Church exists to announce God and his loving care of the world. This is our main challenge."

The dilemma touches upon every aspect of life, and the solution, from the Church's standpoint, hinges not only on a thoroughgoing reform of the Church, but on a personal encounter with Jesus Christ that will empower a renewed Catholic world to proclaim the Gospel with power and burning zeal. In short, the answer lies with the New Evangelization.

In effect, the modern Church must come to grips with the fact that many areas that were once deeply imbued with the Faith no longer are. We see, as Cardinal Angelo Scola of Milan said, the tragedy that "God has been forgotten."

Benedict XVI placed immense importance on the New Evangelization as a major component in the renewal of the Church and as his strategy for Catholics in reaching out to the modern world. Toward that end, in 2011 he created the Pontifical Council for Promoting the New Evangelization.

At the concluding Mass of the Synod on the New Evangelization in October 2012, the pope meditated on the theme of the gathering. He said: "The New Evangelization applies to the whole of the Church's life. It applies, in the first instance, to the ordinary pastoral ministry that must be more animated by the fire of the Spirit, so as to inflame the hearts of the faithful who regularly take part in community worship and gather on the Lord's Day to be nourished by his word and by the bread of eternal life."

The crisis facing Western culture and the response of the New Evangelization were major topics in the general congregations before the conclave. If the reform of the Curia and the questions of governance were receiving significant press time — correctly so — it could be said that the New Evangelization was the single overarching theme of the pre-conclave deliberations.

Cardinal Donald Wuerl of Washington, D.C., who had served as a relator (or chief organizing bishop) during the sessions at the synod in 2012, said in an interview with Catholic News Service:

> Whoever is going to hold the see of Peter, whoever is going to sit
> in Peter's chair, is going to have to see the issues as Blessed John

Paul did, as Benedict did, as the synod did, as I think most of the cardinals do — that is, that we are very, very much like the early Church in relation to the world around us. Christianity is no longer a dominant culture; secularism is the dominant force in the world of culture. So the Holy Father is going to have to be a person whose focus will be on that.

The One They Seek

In the days leading up to the announcement of the start date for the conclave, the media grew increasingly obsessed with the seemingly shifting fortunes of the various cardinals dubbed by experts and pundits as the *papabili*, those with the best chance of being elected. The list had long included some of the most eminent leaders in the Church, such as Cardinal Angelo Scola of Milan; Cardinal Marc Ouellet, the former archbishop of Quebec and now prefect for the Congregation of Bishops; Cardinal Leonardo Sandri of Argentina, head of the Congregation for the Oriental Churches; Cardinal Odilo Scherer of São Paulo; Cardinal Peter Erdö of Budapest, Hungary; and Cardinal Peter Kodwo Appiah Turkson, president of the Pontifical Council for Justice and Peace and former archbishop of Cape Coast in Ghana.

As with many aspects of the conclave coverage, the discussions and speculations were fun for media people, and all over the world people joined in with their predictions, which were about as well-informed as many being made on the networks or in print. The truth was this: very few knew who the cardinals were really considering because they kept their own counsel and understood the seriousness of the election.

As for the cardinals, important as it was to take the time to meditate on the issues facing the Church, they understood that this was merely part of the process for finding from among the College of Cardinals the one best equipped to deal with them.

While eight years had passed since the death of John Paul II and the election of Benedict — a fraction of a moment in the two millennia of the Church — the crises facing the Faith at this instant in time were now somewhat different. The attributes of the pope, however,

---

✠

"A saintly person, or one on their way to sainthood. A person with the physical strength to carry the weight of the papacy. A person who also has the qualities to make him approachable, acceptable to those in search of God, and who approach the Church. Also someone with management qualities that can help govern the Church."

— CARDINAL LEONARDO SANDRI, PREFECT,
CONGREGATION FOR THE ORIENTAL CHURCHES

---

had remained in many ways broadly the same since Saint Peter. They changed only to the degree that they would be applied to this particular historical moment.

Cardinal Oswald Gracias of Mumbai, India, said to the Catholic News Service, "When I take part in the conclave, I will look for one who — irrespective of where he comes from — is very holy, very intelligent, and has really a world vision, a breadth of vision, a person of compassion, who can reach out to people, and a person with courage, unafraid to speak the truth and face criticism for the sake of the Gospel."

Other cardinals had similar lists of traits and strengths. Collectively, certain characteristics emerged as clear-cut in the comments of the cardinals:

- First, the next pope must be someone with a genuine sense of the universal Church.
- Second, the pope must have a good pastoral sense.
- Third, he must be a gifted administrator and must be a reformer.
- Fourth, the new pope must be fully committed to the New Evangelization and be a natural evangelist.
- Fifth, he must be a person of prayer and holiness.

A Universal Vision

The next pope had to be someone who grasps that the Catholic Church is everywhere, from the sophisticated metropolises of New York and Milan, Italy, to the poorest parts of Kinshasa, Congo, and

Manila, Philippines. As the Vicar of Christ, the next pope will carry not only the pastoral care of the Church on his shoulders, but also the spiritual welfare of the entire planet. He will need the strength to be the center of unity for the world's more than one billion Catholics.

The cardinals could not afford a narrow Eurocentric, Western vision of the modern world and the human condition. While Europe still has a Catholic population of 285 million, more than a quarter of global Catholicism, Latin America is home to 42 percent of the world's Catholics, and, as we have seen, Catholicism is growing steadily in Asia and Africa. To think, therefore, that the concerns of European or American Catholics should outweigh those of their sisters and brothers elsewhere would be a betrayal of the Gospel.

The cardinals were ready to consider candidates from beyond Europe. Up until the election of John Paul II, there had not been a non-Italian pope in 422 years. And there has not been a non-European pope since Gregory III, a Syrian, who served from 731 to 741. The last pope from Africa was St. Gelasius I, who reigned from 492 to 496.

Many observers, and many cardinals, expressed the belief that the Church and the world were ready for someone from beyond Europe. Cardinal Turkson told The Associated Press, "I think in a way the Church is always and has forever been ready for a non-European pope." Cardinal Theodore McCarrick, retired archbishop of Washington, D.C., and a voter in the 2005 conclave, saw it in terms of basic numerical reality when he spoke with *National Catholic Reporter*: "When you just look at the statistics, two-thirds of the Church is outside the West. That's a movement we must become aware of."

The Argentinian Cardinal Leonardo Sandri, a longtime Vatican official, however, adopted a slightly more cautious tone in an interview with Reuters news service. "We are open to anyone as long he is the best prepared, the best qualified, to face a time that is so difficult for the Church and the world," he said.

Among the minimum qualifications for the role is the ability to speak a variety of languages and to be open to the world's rich cultures and cultural heritages. Virtually all of the cardinals emphasized, though, that geography or national or regional blocs were not a factor

---
✠

"One pope is different from another. When the pope comes, he will (take) his own path, he will do his work, carry out his ministry according to the way he is led by the Spirit. What is important is that whoever is the pope should be a pope for all of us."

— CARDINAL JOHN OLORUNFEMI ONAIYEKAN,
ARCHBISHOP OF ABUJA, NIGERIA]

---

in their discussions and would not influence their vote, as though the Church needed some form of affirmative action for the papacy.

Cardinal Juan Cipriani Thorne of Lima, Peru, told the Catholic News Agency that the new pope will be chosen with God's help and not by nationality. "I think that geography has nothing to do with it," he said. "The right person needs to be sought out with the help of God, regardless of where he is from . . . geographical or political considerations are not going to be part of the conclave."

A Pastor

It goes without saying that the pope must have a good pastoral sense — attentive especially to the poor, marginalized, and defenseless — but many today cite the need for a pastoral pontiff to propel forward the spiritual reform of the Church that began under Benedict XVI, most especially in the Year of Faith. As the leader of the Church, the pope must demonstrate a heart of service, humility, and love, a vision of pastoral service described poignantly by Cardinal Tagle at the synod in October 2012:

> The Church must learn humility from Jesus. God's power and might appears in the self-emptying of the Son, in the love that is crucified but truly saves because it is emptied of self for the sake of others.
>
> The Church is called to follow Jesus' respect for every human person. He defended the dignity of all people, in particular those neglected and despised by the world. Loving his enemies, he affirmed their dignity.
>
> The Church must discover the power of silence. Confronted with the sorrows, doubts, and uncertainties of people, she cannot

pretend to give easy solutions. In Jesus, silence becomes the way of attentive listening, compassion, and prayer. It is the way to truth.

The seemingly indifferent and aimless societies of our time are earnestly looking for God. The Church's humility, respectfulness, and silence might reveal more clearly the face of God in Jesus. The world takes delight in a simple witness to Jesus — meek and humble of heart.

Administrator and Reformer

Clearly, the times call for a pope who is a gifted administrator, willing to be a reformer tackling problems in the Roman Curia, the central government of the Church, and helping it to move beyond any scandal, incompetence, careerism, and infighting. Cardinal Sandri addressed this issue as a manifest need of the next pontificate in an interview with Rome Reports. He said: "The Roman Curia must be at the service of the Petrine ministry and the bishops. From that point of view, it must be organized to serve the pope efficiently, and to serve the whole Church through the College of Bishops, and its members."

In addition, the new pope has to push ahead with the reforms put in place by Benedict to end sex abuse by the clergy, building on his significant progress in this regard.

There is no shortage of administrative experience among the cardinals, both in leading archdioceses with millions of Catholics and in heading key offices in the papal administration. In some cases, cardinals had experience both in the Curia and as shepherds of archdioceses. While this can be a significant plus, it is not an essential element in securing the vote of cardinals. John Paul II had no experience in Rome, but he was a determined reformer of the papal government in the early years of his pontificate. In this sense, Cardinal Pell could declare, in an interview with Catholic News Service: "I think at the moment we need a pope who is an experienced pastoral leader, who has run a diocese and can encourage the Roman Curia in the right direction. What we want is a good pope who will lead us as effectively as possible in these difficult times."

Cardinal Onaiyekan cautioned Catholics, too, about losing perspective on the Church's problems. "I do believe," he told Catholic

News Service, "that very often there's a tendency to exaggerate the gravity and even the moment [importance] of the problems we have in our house today. Anyone who has read Church history knows that there is nothing new on that." He added, "Jesus Christ could have left this Church in the hands of angels; there were enough in heaven to do the job."

An Evangelist

Any new pope must not only support the New Evangelization but must find new and creative ways to implement it. Cardinal Peter Erdö, the archbishop of Budapest, described the essentially Christocentric dimension of this when he told reporters: "I ask myself, who is the active subject for this New Evangelization? We are convinced that the evangelizer above all else is Jesus Christ, the same for the Holy Spirit within our Church, then the whole Church and the Christians. Because to be Christian is an active mission, not just a lifestyle."

Carrying the New Evangelization forward in the encounter between the Church and modernity will not be easy for any pontiff as he confronts the riptides of secularism, materialism, relativism, and atheism. To be sure, an older pope in excellent health could provide dynamic leadership, but the cardinals seemed disposed to a younger man. How *much* younger was tempered by a realistic understanding that a pontificate stretching out for thirty or forty years might not be desirable. Seasoning, a solid temperament, experience, prudence, and wisdom were attributes mentioned repeatedly.

"The task," Cardinal Wuerl told reporters in Rome, "is going to require an enormous amount of physical energy." He added: "More important than the physical energy is the spiritual energy, but you do need a certain amount of physical energy to carry out the task. So I suspect that the next pope could be someone who would be perhaps younger than Cardinal Ratzinger was when he was elected and became Benedict."

Cardinal Wuerl could have listed another desired skill set for the next pope: ease and familiarity with modern technology, most so in using social media. He told reporters in Washington, D.C., before leaving for Rome, that the next pontiff "has to be able to get the

✠

CARDINALS WHO TWEET

Many members of the College of Cardinals have embraced social media, including both Facebook and Twitter. As of the end of February 2012, there were twenty cardinals with Twitter accounts. Their tweets, of course, ended with their entry into the conclave. The numbers of followers varied. Cardinal Dolan has 90,000 followers, Cardinal Ravasi 42,000, Cardinal Scherer 24,000, Cardinal Scola 19,000, and Cardinal O'Malley around 11,000. The rest are under 5,000. The Pope's Twitter account, @ pontifex, was expected to start again after the papal election. The list of Tweeting Cardinals includes:

Cardinal Angelo Bagnasco, archbishop of Genoa, Italy
Cardinal Tarcisio Bertone, Secretary of State, Vatican
Cardinal Timothy Dolan, archbishop of New York
Cardinal Willem Jacobus Eijk, archbishop of Utrecht, Netherlands
Cardinal Nicolás de Jesús López Rodríguez, archbishop of Santo
    Domingo, Dominican Republic
Cardinal Roger Mahony, archbishop emeritus of Los Angeles
Cardinal Lluís Martínez Sistach, archbishop of Barcelona, Spain
Cardinal Wilfred Fox Napier, archbishop of Durban, South Africa
Cardinal Seán Patrick O'Malley, archbishop of Boston
Cardinal Gianfranco Ravasi, president, Pontifical Council for Culture
Cardinal Norberto Rivera Carrera, archbishop of Mexico City
Cardinal Francisco Robles Ortega, archbishop of Guadalajara, Mexico
Cardinal Odilo Scherer, archbishop of São Paulo
Cardinal Angelo Scola, archbishop of Milan, Italy
Cardinal Luis Antonio Tagle, archbishop of Manila, Philippines
Cardinal Jean-Louis Tauran, president, Pontifical Council for
    Interreligious Dialogue
Cardinal Peter Turkson, president, Pontifical Council for Justice and
    Peace
Cardinal Donald Wuerl, archbishop of Washington, D.C.
Cardinal Rubén Salazar Gómez, archbishop of Bogotá, Colombia
Cardinal Christoph Schönborn, archbishop of Vienna

message out using these modern means of communications," such as Twitter, a major social-media platform. Pope Benedict, he noted, "was already opening the doors to that, and I think of the number of cardinals, [including] European cardinals, who are engaged in [the] Web, have blogs and websites and Twitter. That's no longer an American prerogative."

And, of course, the pope must be a true evangelist, proclaiming the Gospel and the truths of the Church joyfully, free of negativity and pessimism. As the Synod of Bishops on the New Evangelization stated:

> There is no room for pessimism in the minds and hearts of those who know that their Lord has conquered death and that his Spirit works with might in history. We approach this world with humility, but also with determination. This comes from the certainty that the truth triumphs in the end. We choose to see in the world the Risen Christ's invitation to witness to his Name. Our Church is alive and faces the challenges that history brings with the courage of faith and the testimony of her many daughters and sons.

Holiness

Finally, the new pontiff must be a person of sound doctrine, prayer, and holiness. These seem at first obvious attributes, but they're more needed than ever in what is already being called a post-Christian era. Likewise, the ability to teach the truths of the Faith clearly is essential, a gift held by both John Paul II and Benedict XVI.

Cardinal Dolan addressed the issue of doctrine in his March 8 blog post. "The 'job description' of the Bishop of Rome," he wrote, "is to *conserve* the faith, the truths of which have been revealed to us by God, especially through his Son, Jesus, faithfully passed on by his

---

"If the pope is a saint, I'm sure it's an enormous advantage."

— Cardinal George Pell,
archbishop of Sydney

Church these past 2,000 years, and to renew the invitation of Jesus to a *change of heart.*"

In the end, then, the next pope — any pope — must be Christ-like, modeling prayerfulness and a thirst for holiness.

In all of this, finally, the Church encounters the central role of the Holy Spirit. Who does the Holy Spirit have in mind to lead the Church in the time after Benedict XVI's pontificate? As Cardinal Ennio Antonelli (who was eligible to vote in the 2013 conclave) famously quipped in the lead up to the 2005 conclave, "The next pope is already chosen by the Holy Spirit, even now, and it's our job to discover him."

PART II

---✦---

"Habemus Papam!": "We Have a Pope!"

Chapter Four

"FROM THE ENDS
OF THE EARTH"

✠

"I announce to you a great joy; we have a pope! The Most Eminent and Most Reverend Lord, Lord Jorge Maria of the Holy Roman Church Cardinal Bergoglio who has taken upon himself the name of Francis."

— CARDINAL JEAN-LOUIS TAURAN,
SENIOR CARDINAL DEACON, MARCH 13, 2013

After several more days of discussion, the assembled cardinals finally took a vote and set the actual start of the conclave for March 12. With that, media interest picked up, reporters from around the world streamed into Rome, and planes packed with pilgrims and the curious headed to Italy.

The first conclave to be held in the age of social media — the one in 2005 had actually predated the rise of Facebook (which was launched in 2004 but was reserved for college-student use until late in 2005) and Twitter — the papal election also generated an Internet obsession with all things related to the work and activities of the cardinals. Over half-a-million people signed up at the "adopt a cardinal" Web site to receive the name of a cardinal for whom they would pray. A text service promised to alert the recipient when a pope had been chosen, and there were apps to watch the chimney of the Sistine Chapel. The chimney also had its own Twitter accounts, @papalsmokestack and @papalchimney, although Catholic bloggers humorously noted that the chimney could not tweet because Vatican security had installed electronic and phone jammers.

On Sunday, March 10, the cardinals dispersed through Rome to say Masses in their titular churches. The result was a scrum between reporters and the faithful as they filled the churches, in particular those that had been assigned to the perceived front-runners. Reporters and photographers descended on the Church of the Twelve Holy Apostles (the Santi XII Apostoli) for the Mass said by Cardinal Angelo Scola, and similar crowds pushed their way into Santa Maria in Traspontina to see Cardinal Marc Ouellet, Santa Maria della Vittoria to see Cardinal Séan O'Malley, and Sant'Andrea al Quirinale to see Cardinal Odilo Scherer. Typical of the day, reporters set upon a couple who received a blessing from Cardinal Scherer for their seventieth wedding anniversary, curious about their reaction to having been blessed by a possible future pope.

And so the process that had started on February 11, with the announcement of Pope Benedict's resignation, moved ahead in earnest on March 12 with the arrival of the cardinals at the Vatican for the start of the conclave. The resignation and the ensuing events had been a formidable spiritual experience for them and for the Church, but with the start of the conclave, the speculation, endless discussion, heated debates, and sensational stories were forgotten. The world would soon turn its eyes to the scarlet procession of the cardinals into the Sistine Chapel to elect the 266th pope.

Established rites of the Church govern the actual conclave and are prescribed in the *Ordo Rituum Conclavis* (*Rites of the Conclave*). It is, to be sure, a juridical undertaking. But the text states that a papal election "is of supreme importance in the life of the people of God in pilgrimage on earth," and so a papal election is also a liturgy, filled with prayer, spiritual reflection, and the entrustment once again of the Church to the guidance of the Holy Spirit. Cardinal Thomas Collins of Toronto expressed this reality well when he told reporters,

> In the whole process there is a great deal that is very human. Discussion, in fact, is required. It's part of the rule of the conclave you must have time to discuss things, think things through. But at the same time it's Divine. There is the praying for the guidance of the Holy Spirit as we make this choice. There are these two dimensions which go together, like faith and reason; that's the way God made us, grace builds on nature. So we need to be attentive to both dimensions. It is something that people some-

✠

There are these two dimensions which go together, like faith and reason; that's the way God made us, grace builds on nature.

— CARDINAL THOMAS COLLINS

times forget when they are thinking of this in terms of who are the contenders, there is a whole political paradigm, it's all understandable, but it misses the point.

That the election of a pope is a spiritual undertaking — and that people often miss that point — was crucial. The cardinals almost universally spoke of the role of the Holy Spirit in the process, and it was for good reason that on the very day that the conclave began, they gathered in Saint Peter's Basilica for the Mass for Electing the Supreme Pontiff (the *missa pro eligendo romano pontifice*) in which the Holy Spirit is invoked.

But first, early Tuesday morning, March 12, the cardinals arrived at the Domus Sanctae Marthae, the residence in the Vatican built by Pope John Paul II to house the cardinals during the conclave (and which is otherwise used as a hotel for guests of the Vatican and visiting prelates). They then headed over to the basilica for the Mass.

The Mass did not have the drama of 2005, when Cardinal Joseph Ratzinger, then Dean of the College of Cardinals and the absolute favorite to be elected, delivered one of the most memorable homilies in modern papal elections, a homily that was seen as his manifesto for a prospective pontificate should he be chosen. This time, Cardinal Angelo Sodano, Dean of the College, gave the homily, drawing applause when he mentioned "the beloved and venerable Pontiff Benedict XVI, to whom we renew in this moment all of our gratitude."

At the end of the Mass, Cardinal Sodano declared: "After having celebrated the divine mysteries, we now enter into conclave to elect the Roman pontiff. The whole Church, united with us in prayer, invokes the grace of the Holy Spirit so that we elect a worthy pastor of the entire flock of Christ."

Around 3:45 p.m. Rome time, the cardinals were transferred from the Domus to the Pauline Chapel in the Vatican Palace. Dominating

—— ✠ ——

After having celebrated the divine mysteries, we now enter into conclave to elect the Roman pontiff.

— FROM THE MASS FOR ELECTING A SUPREME PONTIFF

the chapel are several brooding frescoes by Michelangelo, including the "Crucifixion of Saint Peter." From there, the cardinals began the spellbinding procession — broadcast around the world — from the Pauline Chapel along the Sala Regia and into the Sistine Chapel. Processing behind a cross, the cardinals recited the haunting Litany of Saints, the list of holy men and women from the East and West, and made a series of invocations to Christ with the refrain, "Save us, Lord."

Once the cardinals took their places, they chanted the ancient invocation of the Holy Spirit, *"Veni, Creator Spiritus."*

One by one, the cardinals walked up to the Book of the Gospels that had been placed in the middle of the chapel and took the oath to "faithfully and scrupulously observe" the rules of the conclave, including secrecy regarding its proceedings. Each one also swore that if elected, he would "faithfully fulfill the Petrine ministry as pastor of the universal Church and will strenuously affirm and defend the spiritual and temporal rights as well as the freedom of the Holy See."

When the last cardinal finished his oath, Msgr. Guido Marini, the papal master of ceremonies, quietly declared the venerable command: *"Extra omnes!"* ordering all those not directly taking part in the conclave to leave the Sistine Chapel. In a dramatic moment, the doors of the chapel closed.

The conclave had begun. Each vote was cast beneath Michelangelo's towering masterpiece, "The Last Judgment," painted from 1525 to 1541 and a reminder of the task at hand. Cardinal Napier told Catholic News Service,

> The most solemn, the most difficult, frightening (moment) is when you go with your ballot paper in your hand and hold it up in front of the altar and say, "I call on the Lord Jesus, who will be my judge, to witness that I am voting for the one I believe to be

worthy." That's really a moment of intense emotion, faith, all these emotions come together at that point. If I'm voting for unworthy reasons I'm actually asking Jesus to judge me, to condemn me, so it's a very, very solemn moment.

For the rest of the world, the television coverage of the procession and the opening of the conclave told a tale of antiquity, spiritual beauty, and the awesome duty placed upon the cardinals as they took their oath upon the Gospels before an audience of over one billion people. There remained only to wait for the verdict of the Holy Spirit.

What happened next in the actual voting will be the subject of study and theorizing among Vatican scholars over the next days, weeks, and years as they try to piece together the fortunes of various candidates and explain how the cardinals finally selected the next pontiff. Outside the Chapel, television and Web cameras pointed toward the chimney protruding from the Sistine Chapel and simply awaited the smoke. The excitement generated on Wednesday afternoon when two seagulls landed on the chimneystack typified the waiting. The seagulls became instant social media celebrities.

At 7:06 p.m., on Wednesday, March 13, the crowd in the square went wild. *Fumata bianca* — white smoke — billowed out of the

---

RECENT CONCLAVE BALLOTS AND DAYS

1903: Saint Pius X, 4 days, 7 ballots
1914: Benedict XV, 4 days, 10 ballots
1922: Pius XI, 5 days, 14 ballots
1939: Piux XII, 2 days, 3 ballots
1958: Blessed John XXIII, 4 days, 11 ballots
1963: Paul VI, 3 days, 6 ballots
1978: John Paul I, 2 days, 4 ballots
1978: Blessed John Paul II, 3 days, 8 ballots
2005: Benedict XVI, 2 days, 4 ballots
2013: Francis, 2 days, 5 ballots

chimney of the Sistine Chapel. The smoke poured forth for the next several minutes as word flew across the city and the globe. The conclave was over.

Within minutes, the crowd in the square before Saint Peter's grew to more than 150,000 people praying, singing, cheering, and steadily watching the red curtain on the central window of the loggia for the announcement. At last, at 8:10 p.m., the doors opened and Cardinal Jean-Louis Tauran, the senior cardinal deacon, stepped out. He proclaimed:

> *Annuntio vobis gaudium magnum;*
> *habemus Papam!*
> *Eminentissimum ac Reverendissimum Dominum,*
> *Dominum Georgium Marium*
> *Sanctae Romanae Ecclesiae Cardinalem Bergoglio*
> *qui sibi nomen imposuit Franciscum.*

> I announce to you a great joy;
> we have a Pope!
> The Most Eminent and Most Reverend Lord,
> Lord Jorge Mario
> of the Holy Roman Church Cardinal Bergoglio
> who has taken upon himself the name of Francis.

The cardinal's name in the announcement left the crowd momentarily puzzled, as it was largely unknown to most in the piazza. The same reaction was typical of some on the television networks covering the conclave who either had not caught the name of the cardinal as it was announced or had only a vague notion of who he was. And then Tauran proclaimed the name of the new pope: Francis. The mostly Italian crowd broke into ardent cheering that did not stop until the new pope finally appeared. By then the announcers were able to catch their breath and inform their viewers and listeners that the next successor of Saint Peter was the 76-year-old archbishop of Buenos Aires, Argentina, Jorge Mario Bergoglio.

The surprise of the crowd continued when Pope Francis came into view, a humble, quiet, and ascetic figure. Instead of the traditional gesture of the popes of lifting their arms in a pontifical greeting, the next pope raised only his right hand and gave a gentle wave to the crowd. Not only was he unexpected, so too was what followed when the new Supreme Pontiff gave the apostolic blessing *Urbi et Orbi* ("To the City and the World").

> Brothers and sisters, good evening!
>
> You know that it was the duty of the conclave to give Rome a bishop. It seems that my brother cardinals have gone to the ends of the earth to get one . . . but here we are. . . . I thank you for your welcome. The diocesan community of Rome now has its bishop. Thank you!
>
> And first of all, I would like to offer a prayer for our bishop emeritus, Benedict XVI. Let us pray together for him, that the Lord may bless him and that Our Lady may keep him.

Pope Francis then led the faithful in a recitation of the Our Father, the Hail Mary, and the Glory Be. He then continued:

> And now, we take up this journey: bishop and people. This journey of the Church of Rome which presides in charity over all the Churches. A journey of fraternity, of love, of trust among us. Let us always pray for one another. Let us pray for the whole world, that there may be a great spirit of fraternity. It is my hope for you that this journey of the Church, which we start today, and in which my cardinal vicar, here present, will assist me, will be fruitful for the evangelization of this most beautiful city.
>
> And now I would like to give the blessing, but first — first I ask a favor of you: before the bishop blesses his people, I ask you to pray to the Lord that he will bless me: the prayer of the people asking the blessing for their bishop. Let us make, in silence, this prayer: your prayer over me.

☩

And now, we take up this journey: bishop and people. This journey of the Church of Rome which presides in charity over all the churches.

— Pope Francis

The pope then bowed down humbly as the entire square fell into silence in an unprecedented moment of prayer. He straightened again and declared:

> Now I will give the blessing to you and to the whole world, to all men and women of good will.
>
> Brothers and sisters, I leave you now. Thank you for your welcome. Pray for me and until we meet again. We will see each other soon. Tomorrow, I wish to go and pray to Our Lady, that she may watch over all of Rome. Good night and sleep well!

Pope Francis had been elected on the second day of the conclave on the fifth ballot.

His election was startling, unanticipated, and spiritually overwhelming. He was, from the moment of his election, a pope of many firsts. It was said by the cardinals within a few hours of the conclave that when he had reached the needed seventy-seven votes there had been spontaneous applause in the Sistine Chapel, and when he declared his name would be Francesco, or Francis, the three Franciscan cardinals cheered, but so did the other cardinals. He was the first pope to take the name Francis. He was the first pope from Argentina, the first from South America, the first from the Southern Hemisphere, the first from the Western Hemisphere, the first to be elected from the Society of Jesus, the first non-European since 731.

He was also someone who from the start placed his own stamp on the new pontificate.

The choice of the name was more than merely a first-time appellation for a pope. It gave the cardinals and then the world an important insight to how he intended to govern. As Cardinal Timothy Dolan said in a press conference, the new pope had chosen Francis specifically in honor of Saint Francis of Assisi. The pontiff was declaring to everyone that this was to be a pontificate of humility and service.

He manifested this exquisitely when he returned from the Room of Tears (where the pontiffs change from the traditional scarlet of the cardinal into the papal white) to receive the pledge of obedience from the members of the College of Cardinals. He chose not to sit to receive their obeisance. Instead, he walked down to the floor of the

---

WHAT'S IN A NAME?

Some people wanted to know why the Bishop of Rome wished to be called Francis. Some thought of Francis Xavier, Francis De Sales, and also Francis of Assisi.

I will tell you the story. During the election, I was seated next to the archbishop emeritus of São Paulo and prefect emeritus of the Congregation for the Clergy, Cardinal Claudio Hummes: a good friend, a good friend! When things were looking dangerous, he encouraged me. And when the votes reached two-thirds, there was the usual applause, because the pope had been elected. And he gave me a hug and a kiss, and said: "Don't forget the poor!"

And those words came to me: the poor, the poor. Then, right away, thinking of the poor, I thought of Francis of Assisi. Then I thought of all the wars, as the votes were still being counted, till the end. Francis is also the man of peace.

That is how the name came into my heart: Francis of Assisi.

For me, he is the man of poverty, the man of peace, the man who loves and protects creation; these days we do not have a very good relationship with creation, do we? He is the man who gives us this spirit of peace, the poor man. . . .

How I would like a Church which is poor and for the poor!

— Pope Francis speaking to reporters March 16, 2013

chapel and stood as each cardinal came forward to give their obedience and embrace their new pope. A little later, after spending time in adoration before the Blessed Sacrament in the Pauline Chapel, he stepped out on the loggia and bowed before the People of God for their prayers.

Soon after, he showed his low-key style again, but in a most unusual way. Following his appearance on the loggia as Pope Francis, he and the cardinals made their way back to the Domus Sanctae Marthae for a celebratory dinner. The cardinals were taken over in small buses, but a car and driver stood ready for the pope. Cardinal Dolan explained what happened next:

> So we take the buses over and cardinals kind of wait outside to greet the new Holy Father as he comes back to Domus Sanctae Marthae . . . and as the last bus pulls up, guess who gets off the bus? Pope Francis. So I guess he told the driver, "That's okay. I'll just go with the guys on the bus."

Chapter Five

"IN THIS WAY, THE CHURCH WILL GO FORWARD"

✠

"The Holy Spirit is the soul of the Church, with His life-giving and unifying strength. Of many He makes a single body —the mystical Body of Christ."

— POPE FRANCIS, MARCH 15, 2013

The morning after his election, Pope Francis was up early as usual. At around 8:00 a.m., he kept his promise from the previous evening and set out for the Basilica di Santa Maria Maggiore, the Basilica of Saint Mary Major, the world's oldest church dedicated in honor of the Blessed Mother. In keeping, too, with the simplicity of the night before, the new pontiff waved off a papal motorcade and traveled with a minimal security detail and no police escort. Instead, his driver proceeded to the basilica in the rush-hour traffic of Rome in a car provided by the Vatican gendarmerie — a Volkswagen, not a Mercedes. Accompanying the pope was the prefect of the papal household, Archbishop Georg Gänswein, the longtime private secretary to Pope Benedict XVI, and Msgr. Leonardo Sapienza, R.C.I., regent of the pontifical household.

The pope's choice of the Basilica of Saint Mary Major for his first visit following his election was of great interest to the press, but Fr. Federico Lombardi, the Vatican spokesman, said that the visit was an entirely private one. He added, however, that the basilica holds a special place for the members of the Society of Jesus because it contains the altar on which Saint Ignatius Loyola, the founder of the Jesuits, celebrated his first Mass. The basilica also shelters the ancient icon of the Virgin, *Salus Populi Romani* — Protectress of the Roman People — and the pope, as the Bishop of Rome, wanted to pray before the image for his Roman flock. Pope Francis placed a small bouquet of flowers before the icon, located in the Borghese Chapel, and remained there in prayer for fifteen minutes or so. He then prayed briefly at the main altar and at the tomb of Pope Saint Pius V, a zealously reforming pope of the late sixteenth century, in the so-called Sistine Chapel of the basilica.

Leaving the basilica, he greeted the cheering crowd outside and stopped to give a blessing — the second public blessing of his pontificate — to a pregnant woman. And then to the disbelief of the pilgrims and tourists, who perhaps expected a flashier departure, he climbed back into the car and rode away.

On the way back to the Vatican, he told the driver to make a stop. Prior to the conclave, he had stayed at the Casa del Clero, or more fully the Domus Internationalis Paulus VI. This hotel near Piazza Navona is where Vatican officials who are stationed around the world stay when visiting Rome, as do cardinals, bishops and priests who are guests of the Holy See. To the astonishment of the staff, the pope walked up to the front desk and said he wanted to thank everyone for their kindness over the previous two weeks. He then asked for his luggage and handed them a credit card to pay his bill, politely reminding them to include his phone calls. He did this, Fr. Lombardi later said, to give "a good example of what priests and bishops should do."

Pope Francis returned to the Domus Sanctae Marthae, which would remain his home base while the papal apartments were made ready. He met with Vatican officials to prepare for various events, including his installation Mass on March 19, and then had lunch at the Domus, dining with the general community rather than in private.

In the afternoon, the pope went to the Sistine Chapel to celebrate the *Missa pro Ecclesiae* (Mass for the Church) with the cardinal electors. The liturgy, which would include his first homily as pope, was much anticipated. He entered the chapel carrying the same pastoral staff used by Pope Benedict XVI, but he had declined one of the fine mitres from the sacristy of the basilica, preferring the one he typically wore, a simpler mitre trimmed in brown in honor of Saint Francis. Similarly, the evening before, when he dressed in the Room of Tears after his election, he had refused one of the bejewelled pectoral crosses from the sacristy in favor of the pectoral cross he arrived with, a simple silver cross reportedly based on Marc Chagall's "White Crucifixion" at the Chicago Art Institute.

At the conclusion of the Gospel, he did not deliver the homily from his chair. Rather, like a simple homilist, the pope walked to the ambo, focused on the readings for the Mass, and spoke extemporaneously.

In these three readings [Isaiah 2:2-5; 1 Peter 2:4-9; Matthew 16:13-19], I see a common element: that of movement. In the first reading, it is the movement of a journey; in the second reading, the movement of building the Church; in the third, in the Gospel, the movement involved in professing the faith. Journeying, building, professing.

Journeying. "O house of Jacob, come, let us walk in the light of the Lord" (Is 2:5). This is the first thing that God said to Abraham: Walk in my presence and live blamelessly. Journeying: our life is a journey, and when we stop moving, things go wrong. Always journeying, in the presence of the Lord, in the light of the Lord, seeking to live with the blamelessness that God asked of Abraham in his promise.

Building. Building the Church. We speak of stones: stones are solid; but living stones, stones anointed by the Holy Spirit. Building the Church, the Bride of Christ, on the cornerstone that is the Lord himself. This is another kind of movement in our lives: building.

Thirdly, professing. We can walk as much as we want, we can build many things, but if we do not profess Jesus Christ, things go wrong. We may become a charitable NGO [nongovernmental organization], but not the Church, the Bride of the Lord. When we are not walking, we stop moving. When we are not building on the stones, what happens? The same thing that happens to children on the beach when they build sandcastles: everything is

---

Our life is a journey, and when we stop moving, things go wrong."

— POPE FRANCIS

swept away; there is no solidity. When we do not profess Jesus Christ, the saying of Léon Bloy comes to mind: "Anyone who does not pray to the Lord prays to the devil." When we do not profess Jesus Christ, we profess the worldliness of the devil, a demonic worldliness.

Journeying, building, professing. But things are not so straightforward, because in journeying, building, professing, there can sometimes be jolts, movements that are not properly part of the journey: movements that pull us back.

This Gospel continues with a situation of a particular kind. The same Peter who professed Jesus Christ now says to him: You are the Christ, the Son of the living God. I will follow you, but let us not speak of the Cross. That has nothing to do with it. I will follow you on other terms, but without the Cross. When we journey without the Cross, when we build without the Cross, when we profess Christ without the Cross, we are not disciples of the Lord, we are worldly: we may be bishops, priests, cardinals, popes, but not disciples of the Lord.

My wish is that all of us, after these days of grace, will have the courage, yes, the courage, to walk in the presence of the Lord, with the Lord's cross; to build the Church on the Lord's blood which was poured out on the Cross; and to profess the one glory: Christ crucified. And in this way, the Church will go forward.

My prayer for all of us is that the Holy Spirit, through the intercession of the Blessed Virgin Mary, our Mother, will grant us this grace: to walk, to build, to profess Jesus Christ crucified. Amen.

The homily was as different from Benedict's in 2005 as could have been possible. Pope Benedict had delivered his homily from the chair, in Latin, from a text he had written by hand in Latin the evening before. Francis' was entirely spontaneous, given in a pastoral manner with an air that would have been at home in a parish church in Buenos Aires, New York, or Paris. Two popes, two distinct approaches to meditating on the Word of God. Both the Vicars of Christ.

The first Mass celebrated by Pope Francis was also the first opportunity for the many Catholics watching from around the globe to see his searing intensity during the Liturgy of the Eucharist. As he

✠

My wish is that all of us, after these days of grace, will have the cour-age, yes, the courage, to walk in the presence of the Lord.

— POPE FRANCIS

raised the Host and then the Chalice, his eyes narrowed and he gazed intently upon the Eucharist. As much as his gestures of humility and simplicity were helpful in establishing a tone for the pontificate, the way he celebrated the Mass revealed his Eucharistic focus and his love for Christ.

On Friday, Pope Francis met with the College of Cardinals in the Clementine Hall and spoke with them in warm fraternal terms, yet with words that also demonstrated his abiding embrace of the Petrine ministry, which the electors had bestowed upon him. He said:

Brother Cardinals,

This period of the conclave has been filled with meaning not just for the College of Cardinals, but also for all the faithful. During these days we have felt almost palpably the affection and solidarity of the universal Church, as well as the attention of many people who, even if not sharing our faith, look upon the Church and the Holy See with respect and admiration.

From every corner of the earth a heartfelt chorus of prayer was raised by Christian peoples for the new pope, and my first encounter with the crowds filling Saint Peter's Square was an emotional one. With that eloquent image of a praying and joyful populace still fixed in my mind, I would like to manifest my sincere gratitude to the bishops, priests, consecrated persons, young people, families, and to the aged for their spiritual close-ness which is so touching and sincere.

The pope then thanked Cardinals Sodano, Bertone, and Re for their work during the papal transition and the conclave, as well as others, and mentioned that his countryman and retired Vatican librarian Cardinal Mejia, who had fallen ill on the day of the papal election, sent his greetings. (Later that day, Pope Francis paid a surprise visit to the hospital and spent about half an hour with the 90-year-old Cardinal Mejia.)

Pope Francis went on to say:

> I extend an especially affectionate thought, filled with gratitude, to my venerable predecessor, Benedict XVI, who, during the years of his pontificate, enriched and invigorated the Church with his teaching, his goodness, guidance, faith, humility, and his meekness . . . with his gaze always fixed on Christ, the Risen Christ, present and alive in the Eucharist.
>
> Our fervent prayer will always accompany him, our eternal memory, and affectionate gratitude. We feel that Benedict XVI lit a flame in the depth of our hearts, a flame that continues to burn because it will be fanned by his prayers that will continue to sustain the Church on its spiritual and missionary journey.
>
> Dear brother cardinals, this meeting of ours is meant to be the continuation of that intense ecclesial communion we experienced during this period. Animated by a profound sense of responsibility and sustained by a great love for Christ and for the Church, we prayed together, fraternally sharing our feelings, our experiences and reflections.
>
> In this very cordial atmosphere our reciprocal knowledge of one another and mutual openness to one another grew. And this is good, because we are brothers. As someone told me: the cardinals are the Holy Father's priests. But we are that community, that friendship, that closeness, that will do good for every one of us.
>
> That mutual knowledge and openness to one another helped us to be open to the action of the Holy Spirit. He, the Paraclete, is the supreme protagonist of every initiative and manifestation of faith. It's interesting and it makes me think. The Paraclete creates all the differences in the Church and seems like an apostle of Babel. On the other hand, the Paraclete unifies all these differences — not making them equal — but in harmony with one another. I remember a Church father who described it like this: "*Ipse harmonia est*" ["It is harmony itself"]. The Paraclete gives each one of us a different charism, and unites us in this community of the Church that adores the Father, the Son, and him — the Holy Spirit.
>
> Starting from the authentic collegial affection that united the College of Cardinals, I express my desire to serve the Gospel with

renewed love, helping the Church to become ever more in Christ and with Christ, the fruitful life of the Lord. Stimulated by the Year of Faith, all together, pastors and faithful, we will make an effort to respond faithfully to the eternal mission: to bring Jesus Christ to humanity, and to lead humanity to an encounter with Jesus Christ: the Way, the Truth, and the Life, truly present in the Church and, at the same time, in every person. This encounter makes us become new men in the mystery of Grace, provoking in our hearts the Christian joy that is a hundredfold, that is given us by Christ to those who welcome him into their lives.

As Pope Benedict XVI reminded us so many times in his teachings and, finally, with that courageous and humble gesture, it is Christ who guides the Church through his Spirit. The Holy Spirit is the soul of the Church, with his life-giving and unifying strength. Of many he makes a single body — the mystical Body of Christ.

Let us never give in to pessimism, to that bitterness that the devil tempts us with every day. Let us not give in to pessimism, and let us not be discouraged. We have the certainty that the Holy Spirit gives his Church, with his powerful breath, the courage to persevere, the courage to persevere and to search for new ways to evangelize, to bring the Gospel to the ends of the earth.

Christian truth is attractive and convincing because it responds to the deep need of human existence, announcing in a convincing way that Christ is the one Savior of the whole of man and of all men. This announcement is as valid today as it was at the beginning of Christianity, when the Church worked for the great missionary expansion of the Gospel.

Dear brothers, have courage! Half of us are old: I like to think of old age as the seat of wisdom in life. Old people have wisdom because they know they have journeyed through life — like the aged Simeon and Anna in the Temple. It was that wisdom that allowed them to recognize Jesus. We must give this wisdom to young people: like good wine that improves with age, let us give

⊹✠⊹

Let us not give in to pessimism and let us not be discouraged.

— POPE FRANCIS

young people this life's wisdom. I'm reminded of what a German poet said about aging: "*Es ist ruhig, das Alter, und fromm*" — "age is the time of peace and prayer." We need to give young people this wisdom.

You are returning to your respective sees to continue your ministry, enriched by these days so filled with faith and ecclesial communion. This unique and incomparable experience has allowed us to capture all the beauty of the ecclesial reality, which is a reflection of the light of the Risen Christ: one day we shall gaze upon the beautiful face of that Risen Christ.

I commit my ministry, and your ministry, to the powerful intercession of Mary, our Mother, Mother of the Church. Beneath her maternal gaze, may each one of us walk and listen to the voice of her divine Son, strengthening unity, persevering together in prayer, and giving witness to the true faith in the continual presence of the Lord. With these sentiments, sincere sentiments, I impart my apostolic blessing, which I extend to your collaborators and to the people under your pastoral care.

And so the Vatican now began its preparations for the Installation Mass on March 19, the Solemnity of Saint Joseph. Catholics the world over awaited the words of the new pontiff they were just now beginning to know. But as many Catholics were noting in social media, the more they saw and heard of Pope Francis, the more they were coming to love him.

In that light, Fr. Lombardi told the reporters at his briefing on Friday that reports were flooding into Rome of Catholics in Argentina suddenly returning to the Sacrament of Reconciliation.

Chapter Six

"BE PROTECTORS
OF GOD'S GIFTS!"

⊹

*Jesus said to Simon Peter, "Simon, son of John, do you love me more
than these?" He said to him, "Yes, Lord, you know that I love you."
He said to him, "Feed my lambs."*

— JOHN 21:15

By the morning of March 15 and Pope Francis's planned audience
that day with the cardinals in the Clementine Hall, the entire
world was talking about the new pope's first full day, his visit to Santa
Maria Maggiore and, unsurprisingly, his stop at his hotel and his
mission of mercy to his friend in the hospital. He was, put simply, a
media sensation, and social media, both secular and Catholic, was on
fire with tweets, Facebook updates, and blog posts about every move,
word, and gesture. The new pontiff everywhere took people aback,
and many were ecstatic at the choice of the cardinals.

The next day, it seemed as if every journalist and photographer
in Rome had packed into the Paul VI Audience Hall for his or her
first audience with the new pope. The pope thanked the media members for their work over the previous weeks and assured them of the
gratitude of the Church for their efforts. At the same time, he asked
them always to try to "understand more fully the true nature of the
Church, as well as her journey in this world, with her virtues and her
sins, and to know the spiritual concerns which guide her and are the
most genuine way to understand her." He added:

> Historical events almost always demand a nuanced interpreta-
> tion, which at times can also take into account the dimension of
> faith. Ecclesial events are certainly no more intricate than politi-
> cal or economic events! But they do have one particular underly-

ing feature: they follow a pattern which does not readily correspond to the "worldly" categories which we are accustomed to use, and so it is not easy to interpret and communicate them to a wider and more varied public.

The Church is certainly a human and historical institution with all that that entails, yet her nature is not essentially political but spiritual: the Church is the People of God, the Holy People of God making its way to encounter Jesus Christ. Only from this perspective can a satisfactory account be given of the Church's life and activity.

Christ is the Church's pastor, but his presence in history passes through the freedom of human beings; from their midst one is chosen to serve as his Vicar, the Successor of the Apostle Peter. Yet Christ remains the center, not the Successor of Peter: Christ, Christ is the center. Christ is the fundamental point of reference, the heart of the Church. Without him, Peter and the Church would not exist or have reason to exist.

As Benedict XVI frequently reminded us, Christ is present in the Church and guides her. In everything that has occurred, the principal agent has been, in the final analysis, the Holy Spirit. He prompted the decision of Benedict XVI for the good of the Church; he guided the cardinals in prayer and in the election.

It is important, dear friends, to take into due account this way of looking at things, this hermeneutic, in order to bring into proper focus what really happened in these days.

The following morning, Pope Francis said Mass in Saint Anne's Church, nestled just inside the Vatican's Saint Anne's Gate. The Church of Saint Anne in Vatican (*Sant'Anna in Vaticano*) is the small parish church of Vatican City, and its parishioners are made up of the women and men who work in the Vatican City State. The pope's homily was again extemporaneous, and then he amazed and

---

The Church is certainly a human and historical institution with all that that entails, yet her nature is not essentially political but spiritual.

— Pope Francis

delighted the huge crowd outside by processing out of the church and turning to greet those who had just been at the Mass just as would any parish priest anywhere. His homily had as its theme the mercy of Jesus.

This was the central theme also of his Angelus message a little later. His first Angelus as pope drew a crowd of 300,000 people, and he spoke to them both off the cuff and from a prepared text. Of Jesus's mercy, he said:

> We need to understand God's mercy well, this merciful Father who has such patience. . . . Think of the prophet Isaiah who asserts that even if our sins were scarlet red, God's love would make them white as snow. That is beautiful [this aspect of mercy] . . . the problem is that we get tired, we don't want to, we get tired of asking forgiveness. Let us never get tired. Let us never get tired. He is the loving Father who always forgives, who has that heart of mercy for all of us.

On Tuesday, March 19, the solemnity of Saint Joseph, Pope Francis officially inaugurated his pontificate with a Mass in Saint Peter's Square. The enormous crowd, estimated at more than 200,000, exploded with cheers when the pope rode around the square in an open vehicle and waved. He gave a kiss and a blessing to many of the children and babies, and even stopped, got out of the vehicle, and blessed a disabled man. He then vested and descended into the Confession — Saint Peter's tomb beneath the high altar — where he prayed with the ten patriarchs and major archbishops of the Eastern-rite Catholic Churches who were there to express their communion with the Holy Father. Then, he was presented with the symbols of his office — the pallium, the Ring of the Fisherman — which had rested on Saint Peter's tomb overnight.

Just before the start of the Mass, the pallium was placed on the pope's shoulders as a sign of his authority, and the ring, with the image of Saint Peter holding the keys, was placed upon the ring finger of his right hand. Finally, he received the obedience of six cardinals representing the entire College of Cardinals, two from each order of the College — cardinal bishops, priests, and deacons.

Pope Francis's homily was in the style that he had shown in his very first homily a few days before. Rather than a complex theological discourse, he preferred to deliver a homily that was simple but not simplistic, centered on the readings (2 Samuel 7:4-5a,12-14a, 6; Psalm 88; Romans 4:13,16-18,22; Matthew 1:16,18-21,24a), and offered a meditation on protection and the place of Saint Joseph in the Church.

Dear Brothers and Sisters,

I thank the Lord that I can celebrate this holy Mass for the inauguration of my Petrine ministry on the solemnity of Saint Joseph, the spouse of the Virgin Mary and the patron of the universal Church. It is a significant coincidence, and it is also the name day of my venerable predecessor: we are close to him with our prayers, full of affection and gratitude.

I offer a warm greeting to my brother cardinals and bishops, the priests, deacons, men and women religious, and all the lay faithful. I thank the representatives of the other churches and ecclesial communities, as well as the representatives of the Jewish community and the other religious communities, for their presence. My cordial greetings go to the heads of state and government, the members of the official delegations from many countries throughout the world, and the diplomatic corps.

In the Gospel we heard that "Joseph did as the angel of the Lord commanded him and took Mary as his wife" (Mt 1:24). These words already point to the mission which God entrusts to Joseph: he is to be the *custos*, the protector. The protector of whom? Of Mary and Jesus; but this protection is then extended to the Church, as Blessed John Paul II pointed out: "Just as Saint Joseph took loving care of Mary and gladly dedicated himself to Jesus Christ's upbringing, he likewise watches over and protects Christ's Mystical Body, the Church, of which the Virgin Mary is the exemplar and model" (*Redemptoris Custos*, 1).

How does Joseph exercise his role as protector? Discreetly, humbly and silently, but with an unfailing presence and utter fidelity, even when he finds it hard to understand. From the time of his betrothal to Mary until the finding of the twelve-year-old Jesus in the Temple of Jerusalem, he is there at every moment with loving care. As the spouse of Mary, he is at her side in good times and bad, on the journey to Bethlehem for the census and

---

✠

God does not want a house built by men, but faithfulness to his word, to his plan.

— Pope Francis

---

in the anxious and joyful hours when she gave birth; amid the drama of the flight into Egypt and during the frantic search for their child in the Temple; and later in the day-to-day life of the home of Nazareth, in the workshop where he taught his trade to Jesus.

How does Joseph respond to his calling to be the protector of Mary, Jesus, and the Church? By being constantly attentive to God, open to the signs of God's presence and receptive to God's plans, and not simply to his own. This is what God asked of David, as we heard in the first reading. God does not want a house built by men, but faithfulness to his word, to his plan. It is God himself who builds the house, but from living stones sealed by his Spirit.

Joseph is a "protector" because he is able to hear God's voice and be guided by his will; and for this reason he is all the more sensitive to the persons entrusted to his safekeeping. He can look at things realistically, he is in touch with his surroundings, he can make truly wise decisions. In him, dear friends, we learn how to respond to God's call, readily and willingly, but we also see the core of the Christian vocation, which is Christ! Let us protect Christ in our lives, so that we can protect others, so that we can protect creation!

The vocation of being a "protector," however, is not just something involving us Christians alone; it also has a prior dimension which is simply human, involving everyone. It means protecting all creation, the beauty of the created world, as the Book of Genesis tells us and as Saint Francis of Assisi showed us. It means respecting each of God's creatures and respecting the environment in which we live.

It means protecting people, showing loving concern for each and every person, especially children, the elderly, those in need, who are often the last we think about. It means caring for one another in our families: husbands and wives first protect one another, and then, as parents, they care for their children, and children themselves, in time, protect their parents. It means building sincere friendships in which we protect one another in trust, respect, and goodness. In the end, everything has been entrusted to our protection, and all of us are responsible for it. Be protectors of God's gifts!

Whenever human beings fail to live up to this responsibility, whenever we fail to care for creation and for our brothers and sisters, the way is opened to destruction, and hearts are hardened. Tragically, in every period of history there are "Herods" who plot death, wreak havoc, and mar the countenance of men and women.

Please, I would like to ask all those who have positions of responsibility in economic, political, and social life, and all men and women of goodwill: let us be "protectors" of creation, protectors of God's plan inscribed in nature, protectors of one another and of the environment. Let us not allow omens of destruction and death to accompany the advance of this world!

But to be "protectors" we also have to keep watch over ourselves! Let us not forget that hatred, envy, and pride defile our lives! Being protectors, then, also means keeping watch over our emotions, over our hearts, because they are the seat of good and evil intentions: intentions that build up and tear down! We must not be afraid of goodness or even tenderness!

Here I would add one more thing: caring, protecting, demands goodness, it calls for a certain tenderness. In the Gospels, Saint Joseph appears as a strong and courageous man, a working man, yet in his heart we see great tenderness, which is not the virtue of the weak, but rather a sign of strength of spirit and a capacity for concern, for compassion, for genuine openness to others, for love. We must not be afraid of goodness, of tenderness!

Today, together with the feast of Saint Joseph, we are celebrating the beginning of the ministry of the new Bishop of Rome,

---

Let us be "protectors" of creation, protectors of God's plan inscribed in nature.

— POPE FRANCIS

L'Osservatore Romano photo

POPE FRANCIS

JORGE BERGOGLIO (LEFT), NOW POPE FRANCIS, IS SEEN ALONGSIDE HIS BROTHER OSCAR AFTER RECEIVING FIRST COMMUNION IN THIS 1942 PHOTO, COURTESY OF THE POPE'S SISTER MARIA ELENA.

A YOUNGER JORGE MARIO BERGOGLIO (BACK, SECOND FROM LEFT) AND HIS FAMILY MEMBERS ARE
SEEN IN THIS UNDATED PHOTO.

FATHER BERGOGLIO PREACHING IN AN UNDATED PHOTO.

CARDINAL JORGE MARIO BERGOGLIO (RIGHT), NOW POPE FRANCIS, OFTEN TRAVELED BY SUBWAY IN BUENOS AIRES, ARGENTINA.

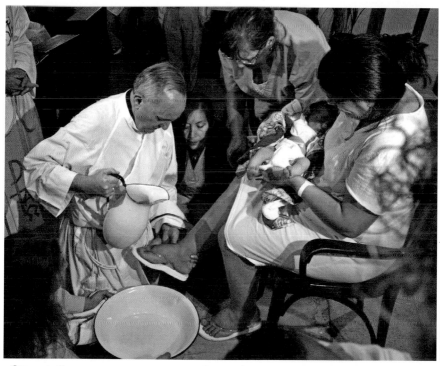

CARDINAL BERGOGLIO, THE ARCHBISHOP OF BUENOS AIRES, WASHES THE FEET OF AN UNIDENTIFIED WOMAN ON HOLY THURSDAY AT THE BUENOS AIRES' SARDA MATERNITY HOSPITAL, MARCH 24, 2005.

POPE FRANCIS APPEARS FOR THE FIRST TIME ON THE CENTRAL BALCONY OF SAINT PETER'S BASILICA, AT THE VATICAN, MARCH 13, 2013.

POPE FRANCIS LEAVES THE SISTINE CHAPEL AFTER BEING ELECTED POPE AND SHORTLY BEFORE APPEARING FOR THE FIRST TIME ON THE CENTRAL BALCONY OF SAINT PETER'S BASILICA.

Pope Francis greets people gathered outside Saint Anne's Church after celebrating Mass at the church within the Vatican on March 17, 2013.

POPE FRANCIS USES INCENSE AS HE CELEBRATES HIS INAUGURAL MASS IN SAINT PETER'S SQUARE ON MARCH 19, 2013.

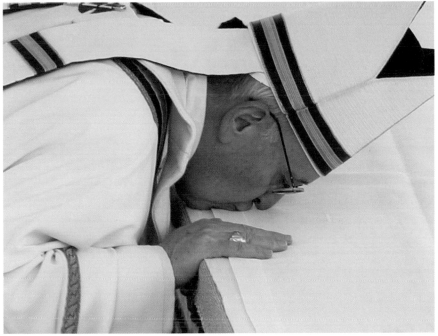

POPE FRANCIS KISSED THE ALTAR AS HE LEAVES AFTER CELEBRATING HIS INAUGURAL MASS.

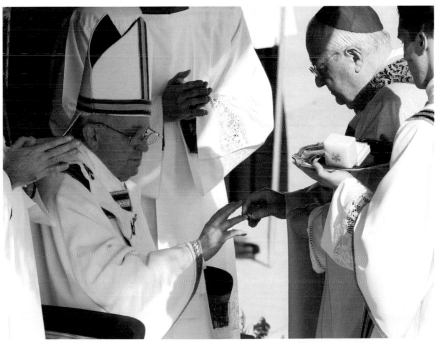

POPE FRANCIS RECEIVES HIS FISHERMAN'S RING FROM CARDINAL ANGELO SODANO, DEAN OF THE COLLEGE OF CARDINALS.

Pope Francis during his inaugural mass.

Saint Peter's Square during Pope Francis's inaugural Mass on March 19, 2013.

©ServizioFotografico OR/CPP

Pope Francis prays before an icon of Mary during a private visit to the fifth-century Basilica of Saint Mary Major.

POPE FRANCIS NEAR THE REPLICA OF THE GROTTO OF LOURDES IN THE VATICAN GARDENS.

the Successor of Peter, which also involves a certain power. Certainly, Jesus Christ conferred power upon Peter, but what sort of power was it? Jesus's three questions to Peter about love are followed by three commands: feed my lambs, feed my sheep.

Let us never forget that authentic power is service, and that the pope too, when exercising power, must enter ever more fully into that service which has its radiant culmination on the Cross. He must be inspired by the lowly, concrete, and faithful service which marked Saint Joseph, and, like him, he must open his arms to protect all of God's people and embrace with tender affection the whole of humanity, especially the poorest, the weakest, the least important, those whom Matthew lists in the final judgment on love: the hungry, the thirsty, the stranger, the naked, the sick, and those in prison (cf. Mt 25:31-46). Only those who serve with love are able to protect!

In the second reading, Saint Paul speaks of Abraham, who, "hoping against hope, believed" (Rom 4:18). Hoping against hope! Today, too, amid so much darkness, we need to see the light of hope and to be men and women who bring hope to others. To protect creation, to protect every man and every woman, to look upon them with tenderness and love, is to open up a horizon of hope; it is to let a shaft of light break through the heavy clouds; it is to bring the warmth of hope! For believers, for us Christians, like Abraham, like Saint Joseph, the hope that we bring is set against the horizon of God, which has opened up before us in Christ. It is a hope built on the rock, which is God.

To protect Jesus with Mary, to protect the whole of creation, to protect each person, especially the poorest, to protect ourselves: this is a service that the Bishop of Rome is called to carry out, yet one to which all of us are called, so that the star of hope will shine brightly. Let us protect with love all that God has given us!

I implore the intercession of the Virgin Mary, Saint Joseph, Saints Peter and Paul, and Saint Francis, that the Holy Spirit may accompany my ministry, and I ask all of you to pray for me! Amen.

The pontificate of Pope Francis was now underway.

PART III

---⊹---

Tu Es Petrus: You Are Peter

Chapter Seven

A TRUE *PORTEÑO*

———————— ✠ ————————

"[Christ] saw the tax collector and, because he saw him through the eyes of mercy and chose him, he said to him: Follow me."

— Venerable Bede, Homily 21,
"Christ's Call of Saint Matthew"

On the night of his election, Pope Francis declared, "You know that it was the duty of the conclave to give Rome a bishop. It seems that my brother cardinals have gone to the ends of the earth to get one."

For anyone who has stood at the very tip of Argentina, in the remote archipelago of Tierra del Fuego, and gazed toward Antarctica to the south, there is truly a sense of the place being at *el fin del mundo*, the end of the world.

Pope Francis was also referring, of course, to the stunning distance between Italy and Argentina, between Rome and Buenos Aires. As noted, Francis is the first pope of the New World, the first from Latin America, and the first from the Southern and Western Hemispheres. But to state an obvious fact, he is also the first pope from Argentina.

Jorge Mario Bergoglio grew up in Argentina, studied for the Society of Jesus there, served as a priest there, and then was an auxiliary bishop there. He was the archbishop of Buenos Aires from 1998 until his election as pope. Although he studied in Chile, Spain, and Germany, and has made many visits to Rome as a cardinal, his entire life and ministry has taken place within the specific context of Argentina — specifically Buenos Aires — and the Church there.

La Argentina

The name Argentina is derived from the Latin *argentum*, silver, and it seemed an apt name for the region to the sixteenth-century Spanish and Portuguese explorers who sailed along the *Rio de la Plata*, the "River of Silver," in search of silver. The rumors of rich silver mines proved false, but the name Argentina stuck. It was first used in print in 1602 when the Spanish priest and explorer Martín del Barco Centenera published *La Argentina*, his poem recounting his two decades of exploration in the region.

Argentina is situated like a rough triangle on the southern tip of South America and is bordered by Chile and the towering Andes Mountains to the West, Uruguay and Brazil to the northeast, Paraguay and Bolivia to the north, and the Atlantic Ocean to the east. It is staggeringly diverse geographically, with the mountains and puna — or montane grasslands — in the west, the rugged coastline in the east, subtropical forests, the Pampas Wetlands, the sprawling grasslands called the Pampas — home to the famous Argentinian cowboys, the gauchos — and the region of Patagonia, with its own steppes and glaciers pointing southward toward Tierra del Fuego and Antarctica beyond. A third of the country's population of forty million live in the capital, Buenos Aires, and there are entire stretches of the country, as in Patagonia, that are only thinly populated.

The faith first arrived in the region with several priests who sailed with the explorer Ferdinand Magellan. Although they celebrated Mass there on April 1, 1519, actual missionary work did not begin until 1530, coinciding with the efforts of Spanish officials to establish colonial domination. Pedro de Mendoza founded the port-side city of Buenos Aires in 1536, but the site was soon abandoned owing to the attacks of the local inhabitants. The Church, meanwhile, began to lay the groundwork for diocesan organization in the 1540s.

Buenos Aires was reestablished in 1580, although it did not become the capital of the Spanish viceroy until 1776. In 1816, after a six-year war, Argentina won its independence from Spain, thanks in large measure to the leadership of General José San Martin. The Church enjoyed good relations with the government of the newly independent Argentina, as is evident, for example, in military leader General Manuel

Belgrano's insistence on assigning many priests as chaplains to help his troops maintain their faith. Argentine leaders also encouraged the Catholic faithful to take part in the devotion to Mary under her title of Our Lady of Luján, including a massive celebration at her shrine near Buenos Aires in thanksgiving for independence.

The next decades, sadly, brought frequent troubles from dictatorships and civil wars, and the Church suffered from repressive regimes and the anticlerical policies of liberal governments. Nevertheless, Argentina grew into a prosperous nation from the latter part of the 1800s, and immigration began to increase steadily, giving the country its rich cultural diversity. Between 1870 and 1914, the population grew from two million to eight million. Buenos Aires assumed much of its distinctive beauty, and over time the melting pot of the older families in the country and the newer immigrants created a unique culture epitomized by the term *porteño* for the inhabitants of Buenos Aires.

The word *porteño* is taken from the full name of the original settlement of Puerto de Santa Maria de los Buenos Ayres, which became Buenos Aires. *Puerto* means *port* in Spanish, and *porteño* captures a sense of pride in the rich heritage that flows from the mélange of cultures in the great metropolis where virtually everyone has come from somewhere else. The *porteños* are mostly second or third generation, with the majority being of Old World descent, primarily from Italy. There is an old saying among the people of Buenos Aires that "a *porteño* is an Italian who speaks Spanish, lives like a Frenchman, and wants to be an Englishman." Most Italian immigrants headed to the United States in the great tides of immigration of the late 1800s and early 1900s, but many went to Argentina. Among them were the Bergoglios.

A Child of Flores

The barrio, or district, of Flores, is located today in the central part of Buenos Aires, but in the nineteenth century it was a green suburb where the wealthy built country houses. Incorporated into the capital in 1888, it is known for its ornate Italianate architecture and has been immortalized in the tango song "*San José de Flores.*"

As the city grew around it, the district — officially called San José de Flores — settled down into a middle-class area, with most of the commercial life centered around the train station on Rivadavia Avenue and the Basilica de San José de Flores, built in 1831. Immigrants poured in, and it was soon one of the largest middle-class barrios in the city, a position it still holds today.

Pope Francis's parents were among those who found their way to the barrio. Both his parents' families emigrated from the Piedmont region of northwest Italy after Benito Mussolini came to power in 1922. According to Pope Francis's sister, their father often said, "The advent of the Fascist regime was the reason why he made up his mind to leave the country." Mario was a railway worker, and he and his wife, Regina Sivori, took up residence in Flores where, their first child, Jorge Mario, was born on December 17, 1936. Of his four siblings — Alberto, Oscar, Marta Regina, and Maria Elena — only Maria Elena, Jorge's junior by eleven years, is still alive. Italy's legal tradition regarding family lines considers the children of Italian citizens to be Italians, regardless of where they are born. As such, the future pope is technically both an Argentinian and an Italian citizen.

Jorge grew up speaking Italian and Spanish as a matter of course, and his mother, especially, instilled in him a love for the Church and the honesty and eagerness to help others that were noted by his teachers. And, he grew up very much a *porteño*.

"If you visit Buenos Aires and have not danced the tango, then you have not been to Buenos Aires," so the saying goes, and true to his heritage, Jorge Mario had a great fondness for the music and the dance. "I like it a lot. It's something that comes from within me," he said in an interview published in the 2010 book *The Jesuit*. Knowledgeable about the history of tango and a fan of many of its great singers, he said that although he danced the tango as a young man, he actually preferred the milonga, the faster country music and dance style that preceded tango.

It comes as no surprise, too, that in a country serious about its *fútbol* (soccer), Pope Francis has long been a fan. In fact, he is member number 88,235 of the San Lorenzo de Almagro soccer club started by a priest to help keep kids off the street. He embraced membership as a *cuervo* (crow) — as the fans of San Lorenzo are called in honor of the black robes worn by Fr. Massa, the founder — but perhaps it was a challenging decision in light of the club's long history of playing hard but giving its fans heartache and frustration.

Another source of heartache for Jorge was, quite possibly, the crush he developed on Amalia Damonte when they were both around the age of twelve. He sent her a letter that included a picture of a house, and told her that he wanted to marry her, and that the house was the one in which they would live. Amalia's parents found the letter and expressed their displeasure, which she then communicated to Jorge. "If you can't marry me," he replied, "then I'll become a priest."

The comment was understandable from a frustrated boy, but it also indicated that a process of discernment was taking place, even at his young age. Christ was calling him, and he was hearing the call.

Jorge settled on a career in chemistry, but his academic hopes slowed down when a pulmonary infection led to cysts, pneumonia, and surgery to remove part of his right lung. Initially, when he was elected pope, it was reported he had only one lung, and some wondered if this would affect his ability to withstand the rigors of the office. Vatican spokesman Fr. Federico Lombardi corrected the record and dismissed the notion that his earlier surgery put him at a disadvantage, saying, "This has never been an obstacle either in his rhythm or for his work, his life, or his pastoral care, as demonstrated by leading a diocese that requires such dedication as that of Buenos Aires."

Though Jorge eventually graduated in chemistry from the University of Buenos Aires, he was by then seriously discerning a call to the priesthood. This was influenced heavily by a deep spiritual experience he had on the feast of Saint Matthew, September 21, 1953, when he was seventeen. After going to confession, he felt God's mercy touch his heart in an overwhelming way. He felt in that instant called to the religious life, to follow the example of Saint Ignatius of Loyola. And so, in the end, he discerned that he was called not only to the priesthood but to the Society of Jesus, the Jesuits.

Ad Majorem Dei Gloriam

Saint Ignatius Loyola founded the Society of Jesus in Paris in 1534, with six companions: Saint Francis Xavier, Blessed Peter Faber, Alphonse Salmeron, Simon Rodríguez, Nicholas Bobadilla, and Diego

Laynez. Loyola and the six gathered in a Benedictine chapel in Montmarte, in Paris, and took vows of chastity and poverty, and a promise to embark, if possible, on a pilgrimage to the Holy Land. The pilgrimage proved impractical, and the group journeyed to Rome to offer itself to the service of the papacy. Pope Paul III gave formal approval for the new religious order on September 27, 1540, and Ignatius was elected the first general of the Society of Jesus.

The order's motto — *Ad majorem Dei gloriam* ("For the Greater Glory of God") — is attributed to Loyola and captures his vision for the order as the men embarked on their missionary efforts around the globe. Beyond the vows of chastity, obedience, and poverty, the Jesuits take a special oath of obedience to the Holy See, placing themselves entirely at the disposal of the popes, going forth immediately and without question wherever he might command.

Ignatius wanted priests who were superbly educated and highly disciplined. The men were prohibited from accepting any preferment or office unless specifically pressed upon them by the pope, and their habit was to be simple and without any distinction. They quickly became the vanguard for much of the Catholic Reformation, bringing reform to the Church in Central and Western Europe.

The Society of Jesus, with its highly educated members, emerged as one of the foremost teaching orders: by the end of the sixteenth century the Jesuits had founded more than a hundred colleges. The men worked outside of academia, too, preaching, giving catechetical instruction, educating the poor, and bolstering the faith wherever it was under threat. Deeply involved in the missionary campaigns of the Church, the Society encountered often-bitter opposition not only from native peoples or governments but from colonial regimes, other orders, secular clergy, and business elements who resented the Jesuit efforts to keep indigenous populations free from exploitation. Nevertheless, the Jesuits had enormous success in Japan, China, North America, and South America, and prior to their suppression in 1773 were operating fourteen universities, some six hundred colleges, and nearly two hundred seminaries.

After being suppressed by Pope Clement XIV in 1773 because of the threats of European powers (many of them Catholic) that hated

---

✠

Ad majorem Dei gloriam ("For the Greater Glory of God").

— MOTTO OF THE SOCIETY OF JESUS

---

the Jesuit's devotion to the Holy See, the Society was reconstituted in 1814 by Pope Pius VII at the end of the Napoleonic Wars. The appeal of the reborn Jesuits caught on throughout the first half of the nineteenth century and their numbers steadily increased. Today, they remain the largest religious order in the Church, with more than 18,000 members.

The first Jesuit missionaries to land in what became Argentina arrived in 1586. After establishing a college in Córdoba, they set out to bring the Gospel to the indigenous peoples of the Southern Cone region. The missions met with success, and the order sent in more members, so that by the start of the seventeenth century there were more than one hundred Jesuits active among the native peoples starting missions and schools. They had settlements in Buenos Aires, Tucumán, Asunción, and Mendoza, and in 1622 they founded the Universidad de Córdoba, one of the first universities in South America.

The Jesuit Reductions — settlements that brought native people together in a protective environment — successfully shielded indigenous people from the *encomienda* system of the Spanish colonies that regulated the lives of native people and were rife with injustice. The Reductions, especially those in Paraguay, prospered through the cultivation of sugar, cotton, yerba maté, and other agricultural products, and were so successful that they contributed to the decision of the Spanish to expel the Jesuits in 1767. With the expulsion, the Jesuits lost control of a host of missions and schools across the region.

With the rebirth of the order in 1814, it did not take long for the Jesuits to return to South America in force. They arrived in Argentina in 1837, but were expelled by the dictator Juan Manuel de Rosas in 1841. In 1852, the new leader of Argentina invited them back, and they have never left. As was the case across all of Latin America, the Jesuits were a major presence in the lives of Catholics, running missions and schools, and have been known for their love of the poor.

It was not surprising then, that Jorge Mario was attracted to this order, which would unite his commitment to the religious life and the priesthood with his abiding concern for others and his many intellectual interests.

He entered the Jesuit novitiate at Villa Devoto, Argentina, in 1958, when he was twenty-two, and began the Jesuit's traditionally long and intense period of formation.

The Jesuit novice spends two years in spiritual and intellectual formation centered on prayer, discernment, and the study of the humanities and other relevant subjects. If, after further discernment and the consent of the provincial, a novice is found to have the required levels of maturity and progress, he is invited to take his first perpetual vows and proceed to first studies.

All scholastics — as the Jesuits call candidates for the priesthood after first vows — then complete graduate-level philosophy and theology studies over the course of three years, culminating in a master's degree in philosophy.

The scholastic then proceeds to an apostolic assignment, an integral part of the next step in formation that typically lasts for two or three years and includes teaching in one of the Society's high schools or universities. This time is called regency, and when it concludes the Jesuit asks for permission to embark on studies for the priesthood. Thus begins a three-year program of theological studies, spiritual formation, and preparation for the priesthood that culminates in ordination.

There is still a final period in the formation process, called tertianship, or "third," because it is connected to the first two years of training in the novitiate and implies a third year in the novitiate, with a concentrated focus on spiritual formation. It can range in length from six to nine months and usually takes place three years after ordination. At the end of this decade-long formation program, a Jesuit pronounces his final vows and is a full member of the Society of Jesus.

Jorge Mario progressed through the formation program in Jesuit schools and houses of formation in both Argentina and Chile. He began his novitiate in Chile, where he was trained in the humanities, and then went to the Colegio Máximo San José, San Miguel, Buenos Aires for a licentiate in philosophy (an advanced master's program). He was appointed a professor of literature and psychology in the Colegio de la Inmaculada, Santa Fe, and in Colegio del Salvador, in Buenos Aires.

Having impressed his superiors, he received permission to advance to the program of theology and priestly formation at the Colegio Máximo de San Miguel, in Buenos Aires.

MARY, UNTIER OF KNOTS

During his time in Germany in the early 1980s, Fr. Jorge Mario Bergoglio saw an early eighteenth-century painting by Johann Schmidtner in the Church of Saint Peter am Perlach, in Augsburg. The painting is of the Blessed Virgin Mary under the unusual title of the "Untier of Knots." Devotion to the Blessed Mother under that name dates at least to the early part of the seventeenth century when a priest saved the marriage of a German noble couple by using the image of knots being unraveled to show the way to marital peace. The image of Mary as an untier of knots was first cast by Saint Irenaeus of Lyons when he spoke of the knot of Eve's disobedience being loosed by the obedience of Mary (*Adversus haerses*, Book III, chapter 22).

Years later, the grateful grandson of the married couple donated an altarpiece to the long-dead priest's church, and the painter Schmittdner, being aware of the family story, depicted the Virgin Mary as the *Knotenlöserin*, "Untier of Knots."

Bergoglio was so struck by the work that he purchased a copy and brought it back to Argentina. Through his encouragement, the *Virgen Desatanudos*, as she is known, became increasingly popular, growing even more so after his appointment as Archbishop of Buenos Aires. The Blessed Mother under this title is a source of comfort, strength, and inspiration for those facing the many difficulties — the knots — of life.

Cardinal Bergoglio presented a chalice to Pope Benedict XVI with the image of the Virgin engraved on it, and it was announced that Pope Francis would receive a similar chalice as a gift from the people of Argentina.

Archbishop Ramón José Castellano ordained Jorge Mario to the priesthood on December 13, 1969. Fr. Bergoglio by then was already teaching a long list of subjects, including the humanities, philosophy, literature (one of his favorite authors is Fyodor Dostoyevsky), psychology, and theology in different colleges in Argentina. He partook in further studies from 1969 to 1971 and his tertianship at Alcalá de Henares, Spain, from 1971 to 1972. He was then made master of novices at the Villa Barilari, in San Miguel, Argentina, from 1972 to 1973.

Fr. Bergoglio took his final vows on April 22, 1973, when he was thirty-six years old. By that time, he had so impressed his fellow Jesuits that he was elected provincial of the Society in Argentina that same year. His tenure as provincial from 1973 to 1979 came at a challenging time for the Church.

Liberation Theology

One of the first major challenges that confronted the priest as provincial was the embrace of the theological movement of liberation theology by some Jesuits (and indeed by many priests, men and women religious, and laypeople).

The Church has always offered the unfailing teaching that the Gospel of Jesus Christ is a message of freedom and liberation, specifically liberation from the radical slavery of sin. As such, its aim and its end is to bring freedom from the many different kinds of slavery found in human existence, including those forms of slavery in the cultural, economic, social, and political spheres that all derive ultimately from sin, that establish obstacles to living in the truth, and that deprive women and men of their authentic dignity. The term "liberation" is thus a fundamental one in the Old and New Testaments, and there is legitimacy in examining a "theology of liberation" that reflects on the biblical theme of liberation and freedom, on its practical realization, and on the call for an authentic evangelical spirit that embodies a "preferential option for the poor."

Such an option has found rich expression in recent papal writings, in particular the social encyclicals of Pope John Paul II such as *Laborem Exercens* (On Human Work), *Sollicitudo Rei Socialis* (On Social Concerns), and *Centesimus Annus* ("The Hundredth Year," referring to the great encyclical of Pope Leo XIII, *Rerum Novarum* [On Capital and Labor], that launched modern Catholic social teachings). Liberation is, consequently, a common theme in modern times, but it is one rooted firmly in the authentic teachings of the Church in light of the specific message of revelation and interpreted by the magisterium of the Church.

In the years after the Second Vatican Council, however, there were currents of thought regarding liberation that assumed not liberation from sin and its dehumanizing manifestations in the world, but rather liberation that advocated political, economic, and social revolution, often along clearly Marxist lines. Such a collective set of liberation theologies was first seen at work in Latin America as early as the 1950s and 1960s, growing out of a desire to change the prevailing social structures of the period in Central America and South America where poverty was endemic, where dictatorships oppressed their citizens, and where Western exploitative capitalism was considered in some quarters as the chief cause of a multitude of problems. From the start, theologies of liberation were difficult to define, for such an expression could be understood entirely within the context of the Church's special concern for the poor and the victims of oppression, and a resulting commitment to justice.

As they developed, there were several contradictory theological positions being advanced as "liberation theology" in Latin America and then elsewhere around the world. The precise doctrinal boundaries were not defined well, and their own ambiguities of language left them open to manipulation and misunderstanding. The great risk that attended these approaches was the apparent emphasis on liberation from slavery and oppression in exclusively earthly or temporal forms. In this view, liberation from sin is demoted to a place of secondary importance.

In its most extreme form, the language of liberation theology carried overtones of Marxism and the Marxist revolutionary ideas being promoted throughout Central America by guerrilla movements. For those uneducated in the nuances at work, the language of liberation gave them the sense of freedom to become actively involved in the Marxist movements of Nicaragua and El Salvador, and even to support the dictatorship of Fidel Castro in Cuba and the Soviet Union's exporting of revolutionary communism into the Third World. Turmoil resulted, then, over the ambiguities, the misinterpretations, and the uncertainties as to what liberation theology actually meant.

By the early 1980s the situation had become so tumultuous that Cardinal Joseph Ratzinger, the future Pope Benedict XVI, and at that time the prefect for the Congregation of the Doctrine of the Faith (CDF), issued two instructions on the subject of liberation theology. Both instructions were criticized in the media as placing a chill on theological discourse, but both ultimately made positive contributions to the dialogue by restating the authentic teachings of the Church. The first document was released in 1984, *Libertatis Nuntius* (Instruction on Certain Aspects of the Theology of Liberation), and the second was in 1986, *Libertatis Conscientia* (Instruction on Christian Freedom and Liberation).

Libertatis Nuntius began by recognizing the many positive contributions of the theological reflections on the Gospel's call for liberation. It spoke of the value and validity of the term "theology of liberation" and reiterated unequivocally that there was no intention to deter or discourage efforts to bring about true justice, but the "yearning for justice and for the effective recognition of the dignity of every human being needs, like every deep aspiration, to be clarified and guided." The document was concerned especially about the application of Marxist analysis to the theological question of liberation with the result that "the different theologies of liberation are situated between the 'preferential option for the poor' . . . on the one hand, and the temptation to reduce the Gospel to an earthly gospel on the other."

Libertatis Conscientia was published as a companion document, and it was intended to be read in the context of *Libertatis Nuntius*. It addressed the issues of freedom and conscience in light of the modern experience of oppression and the call for liberation as a universal phenomenon. *Libertatis Conscientia*, however, once more situates liberation in the truth — meaning, in Christ — and calls on all of the faithful to share in the proclamation of authentic liberation and freedom.

In the years after the promulgation of the two documents, there followed the collapse of the Soviet Union and the discrediting of Marxist theory throughout the world as a failed ideology. Many practitioners of the various liberation theologies entered into a dialogue with Vatican officials and found much in common with the authentic vision of Pope John Paul II in his own teachings on liberation and freedom.

Some elements of liberation theology went on to engage in active reformist efforts and the promotion of Catholic efforts at justice and peace in the poorest countries of the world. The promotion of the Gospel and giving voice to the poor, the defenseless, and the oppressed remains a priority for all engaged in active ministry in Africa, Latin America, and Asia, where issues of globalization, AIDS, political instability, and shocking poverty remain daily crises. Other supporters went on to embrace new forms of liberation theology in the areas of feminism, homosexuality, and the environment. It is anticipated that new variations on the theology of liberation will arise in the 21st century, but the two documents of the CDF will remain essential foundations for judging them in light of the Gospel.

In the 1980s, Fr. Bergoglio then, and throughout his future ministry, referenced these two documents as an important component for anyone studying liberation theology.

Back in the early 1970s, however, many priests and religious in Latin America were being drawn to liberation theology. Very early in his own ministry, Fr. Bergoglio distanced himself from it as he saw it as an aberration of the Church's authentic concern for the poor and the call to authentic justice rooted in the Gospel and nurturing an encounter with Jesus Christ. Equally, there was the great danger of having the Church dragged into the realm of politics, and possibly into violent political upheaval and revolution.

The issue of political activism and ideology was brought into the wider discussion of the Society of Jesus's direction, especially in Latin America where liberation theology had been born.

In 1975, Fr. Bergoglio led the delegation of Jesuits from Argentina to the 32nd General Congregation of the Jesuits in Rome. Pope Paul VI met with the general congregation and, while applauding the work of

＋

Regarding "liberation theology": Bergoglio has always referred to the
Instructions of the Congregation for the Doctrine of the Faith. He
has always rejected violence, saying that its price is always paid by
the weakest.

— Fr. Federico Lombardi

---

the Society in caring for the poor and the sick, also stressed the authentic role the Jesuits should have. "Wherever in the Church, even in the most difficult and extreme fields, in the crossroads of ideologies, in the front line of social conflict, there has been and there is confrontation between the deepest desires of man and the perennial message of the Gospel, there too, there have been, and there are, Jesuits," Pope Paul said.

At the end of the gathering, the leaders of the Society of Jesus issued a statement about the role of the Jesuits in the modern world. It declared, "It is to engage under the standard of the cross, in the crucial struggle of our time: the struggle for faith and that struggle for justice which it includes."

Returning home with the statement still in his mind and heart, Fr. Bergoglio was confronted with the task of trying to encourage the priests of his province to seek justice and defend and care for the poor, but in ways that were faithful to the teachings of the Church and grounded fully in authentic charity. He told his brothers in the Society that the price of violence is always paid by the weakest.

His effort made him unpopular with some of his confreres, but his approach was especially important because many priests, ardent supporters of liberation theology, were becoming more and more involved in the bloody political unrest of the times.

The Dirty War

The modern history of Argentina has been challenging, to say the least. After decades of political and economic stability, a financial crisis in the late nineteenth century led to an end of the economic boom times and collapsed the currency. Problems that had been hidden came into plain view: severe disparities in wealth and opportunity, a political system controlled by a virtual oligarchy of the wealthy, a gulf between Buenos Aires and the rest of the country, and acute problems of poverty, overcrowding, and economic exploitation in the cities, especially in Buenos Aires. In a foretaste of worse to come, power came into the hands of the Unión Civica Radical, called the Radicals.

The crises provoked by World War I, the crash of the stock market, and the start of the Great Depression were felt in Argentina, and political and economic unhappiness prompted the military to take action. The generals ousted the Radicals in 1930. Ostensible civilian control was returned in 1932, but in reality a junta, a military committee that picked the leaders of the state, controlled Argentina's government. Meanwhile, the economic problems continued, and by the time that Jorge Mario Bergoglio was growing up, much of the country was in desperate economic trouble. This situation led to two related events.

The first was further crowding in the cities as people from the country and smaller towns went in search of work, to Buenos Aires in particular, creating a political powder keg. Young Jorge Mario would have seen the results of the economic crisis — despairing men and women looking for any kind of job, and hungry children his own age.

The second event was the rise of the young Army officer Juan Perón, elected president in 1946. Perón used an alliance with the Argentinian labor unions to forge a populist movement known as Perónism that was enhanced by his marriage to Eva Duarte, a film and radio actress. Eva, called Evita by the adoring crowds, was one of Perón's greatest assets until her death from cancer in 1952. Three years later, Perón was toppled from power and exiled by the generals.

Its political parties polarized, Argentina faced a new crisis two years after Jorge Mario's ordination. By 1973, the situation had become so unstable that Perón returned to the country after eighteen years and was again elected president. He died the next year and was succeeded by his third wife, María Estela Martinez de Perón, who had been his vice-president. Her government engaged in sharp political oppression and failed to fix the economy. With inflation at 1,000 percent, she was deposed by a military coup in 1976 under the direction of General Jorge Rafael Videla, who was president until 1981.

The new regime was termed the *Proceso de Reorganización Nacional* (National Reorganization Process), or simply the Process, a euphemism for a military dictatorship. Opposed by many elements in Argentina, especially the urban guerilla movement *Montoneros* and the Marxist People's Revolutionary Army, the military junta mercilessly attempted to eradicate all opposition. The guerillas, for their part, took part in assassinations and bombings. The terrible time, known as the *Guerra Sucia* — the Dirty War — tormented the country from 1976 until 1983, and Fr. Bergoglio was drawn into its dangers.

Between 13,000 and 30,000 citizens were killed by the regime, chiefly politicians, professors and teachers, students, left-leaning writers, trade unionists, and Marxist guerillas opposed to the dictatorship. The guerillas killed as many as 6,000 military personnel and supporters of the regime.

There was an all-pervading sense of fear and dread. Anyone who angered the regime or was seen as a threat or disloyal could be arrested, and others were killed simply because they were in the wrong place at the wrong time. Adding to the horror, many thousands of those who were arrested became part of the "disappeared ones" (the *Desaparecidos*), including pregnant women whose babies were taken and given to military families without children. (The effort to uncover the identity of these children, now adults, is ongoing and a source of tension in the country.) Many of the disappeared were never seen again, dragged away in the middle of the night, tortured at sites such as the infamous Navy Mechanics Schools, and killed, their corpses sometimes mutilated. Officers in charge took some victims on *vuelos de la muerte* — flights of death — tossing the condemned, still living, out of planes to dispose of them in the Atlantic.

During the terrible events of the Dirty War, Fr. Bergoglio tried to keep his priests safe while walking a fine and dangerous line with the government even as he responded to the crushing needs of so many laypeople trapped in a dictatorship that could torture and kill them at will. The dictatorship targeted a number of his priests because of their associations with the guerillas and their open opposition to the government.

Some of the priests were advocating taking up arms and entering into the bloody struggle. Fr. Jorge's answer was simple: we are priests and cannot become guerillas or revolutionaries. When some priests refused to obey him as superior, he had no choice but to impose penalties, even removing them from the Society of Jesus if necessary. It was a difficult decision to be sure. He repeatedly urged the priests of the province not to give in to the temptation to take up arms and surrender their lives to violence and hatred.

Years later, after Bergoglio had been named the archbishop of Buenos Aires, some human rights groups accused him of not doing enough to resist the regime, and there were even allegations that he colluded with the dictators. The accusers point to the case of the 1976 kidnapping and torture of two of his Jesuits, Orlando Yorio and Francisco Jalics, in which Bergoglio supposedly turned a blind eye. The two were active in a *favela*, or slum, of Buenos Aires and were insistent in their radical teachings. Fr. Bergoglio asked them to cease. According to a statement by Fr. Jalics, after the arrest of a lay worker who had joined the guerillas, the two were suspected by the regime of being collaborators. They were arrested and taken to the Navy Mechanics School where they spent five harrowing months.

Critics of the Church have claimed that Bergoglio somehow had a hand in their arrest and did nothing to rescue them. This was hardly consistent with a man who grew up in a family that had come to Argentina to escape the oppression of Mussolini. In truth, the Jesuit provincial went to extraordinary lengths behind the scenes to prevent their murder. According to an interview with Fr. Bergoglio in 2005, he convinced the priest who said Mass for the Argentine junta leader Jorge Videla to pretend to be sick so that he could take his place. Bergoglio then said Mass in the general's home, and afterward made a private appeal for mercy. The two priests were subsequently released, but the provincial's effort on behalf of these men might very easily have brought about his own arrest.

The media's recent efforts to repeat the attacks on Bergoglio led the Society of Jesus to release a statement from Fr. Jalics, who is now eighty-five and living in a religious community in Germany (Yorio never returned to the Society and died in Uruguay in 2000). He declared: "After we were freed, I left Argentina. Only years later did we have the chance to discuss what had happened with Fr. Bergoglio, who in the meantime had been named archbishop of Buenos Aires. Afterwards we together celebrated a public Mass and solemnly embraced. I am reconciled to the events and view them from my side as concluded. I wish Pope Francis God's rich blessing for his office."

After Bergoglio's election to the papacy, the Frankfurter *Allgemeine Sonntagszeitung*, a German newspaper, disclosed that during the captivity of the priests Bergoglio wrote a letter to Fr. Jalic's brother saying: "I have lobbied the government many times for your brother's release. So far we have had no success. But I have not lost hope that your brother will soon be released." He added, "I have made this affair MY thing. The difficulties that your brother and I have had over the religious life have nothing to do with it."

It was later learned, too, that Bergoglio regularly hid people on Church property to prevent their arrest and once gave his own identity papers to a man who looked liked him so that he could escape the country.

Meanwhile, the generals, increasingly desperate to win public support, went to war with Great Britain in 1982 for control of the disputed Falkland Islands. The British Armed Forces swiftly defeated the Argentinians and reclaimed the islands. The defeat was a military and political humiliation for the generals, and massive protests began in Buenos Aires and elsewhere across the country. General Videla had already stepped down, and his successor, General Leopoldo Galtieri, resigned. General Reynaldo Bignone came out of retirement to preside over the restoration of democracy. The country now faced a long and difficult recovery.

Unsurprisingly, the allegations surfaced again with the election of Pope Francis. When asked about the old accusations, the Vatican spokesman, Fr. Federico Lombardi, denounced them forcefully, and issued a formal statement on March 15:

> The campaign against Bergoglio is well known and dates back to many years ago. It has been carried out by a publication specializing in sometimes slanderous and defamatory campaigns. The anticlerical cast of this campaign and of other accusations against Bergoglio is well known and obvious.

The charges refer to the time before Bergoglio became bishop [of Buenos Aires], when he was provincial superior of the Jesuits in Argentina and accuse him of not having protected two priests who were kidnapped.

This was never a concrete or credible accusation in his regard. He was questioned by an Argentinian court as someone aware of the situation but never as a defendant. He has, in documented form, denied any accusations.

Instead, there have been many declarations demonstrating how much Bergoglio did to protect many persons at the time of the military dictatorship.

Bergoglio's role, once he became bishop, in promoting a request for forgiveness of the Church in Argentina for not having done enough at the time of the dictatorship is also well known.

The accusations pertain to a use of historical-sociological analysis of the dictatorship period made years ago by left-wing anticlerical elements to attack the Church. They must be firmly rejected.

Regarding "liberation theology": Bergoglio has always referred to the instructions of the Congregation for the Doctrine of the Faith. He has always rejected violence saying that its price is always paid by the weakest.

The Church in Argentina has been criticized over the years for too many leaders remaining silent during the Dirty War. In February 2013, for example, an Argentine court sentenced three former soldiers to life imprisonment for the murder of two priests in 1976 and used the opportunity to declare that Church leaders had all too often "closed their eyes" and some had even colluded with the regime in the murder of left-leaning priests.

The bishops of Argentina issued an apology in 2000 in response to the plea made by Pope John Paul II for all bishops to examine their consciences in preparation for the Jubilee that was held in 2000. The Argentinian bishops asked for forgiveness on behalf of all Argentine Catholics for sins committed by them throughout the South American country's history, and especially during the black years of 1976 to 1983. The bishops wrote:

We have been indulgent with totalitarian postures, hurting democracy. We have discriminated against many brothers without committing ourselves to the defense of their rights. . . . We ask your forgiveness, O God, for the silent responsibility and the effective participation of the Church's children in pushing aside human rights, in tortures and rapes, in intransigent ideologies, and in foolish deaths that bloodied our country.

Acknowledging the failings of some Church leaders in the Dirty War, Bergoglio called on the Church in Argentina to offer public penance for the failings of the past. He was also instrumental in organizing another apology from the Argentine bishops in 2012. It said, in part, "We share everyone's pain and once again ask the forgiveness of everyone we failed or didn't support as we should have."

"With Mercy Chosen"

Fr. Bergoglio's time as provincial for the Jesuits in Argentina ended in 1979, although the country faced four more years of the darkness of the Dirty War. He expected to return to academia and teaching and was quickly appointed dean of the faculty of theology and philosophy at the San Miguel, where he had studied. That same year, he took part in the controversial gathering in Puebla, Mexico, of CELAM (the Latin American Episcopal Council) that included vehement declarations in support of liberation theology. Fr. Bergoglio spoke openly against the movement, and at the conference Pope John Paul II, who opened the event on his trip to Mexico, spoke in words that echoed the plea of Fr. Bergoglio to his priests during the Dirty War. Fr. Bergoglio had said:

He [Christ] unequivocally rejects recourse to violence. He opens his message of conversion to everybody, without excluding the very publicans. The perspective of his mission is much deeper. It consists in complete salvation through a transforming, peace-making, pardoning, and reconciling love. There is no doubt, moreover, that all this is very demanding for the attitude of the Christian who wishes truly to serve his least brethren, the poor, the needy, the emarginated; in a word, all those who in their lives reflect the sorrowing face of the Lord.

✛

The goal of our life is to live with God forever. God who loves us gave us life.

— SAINT IGNATIUS LOYOLA

Through the 1980s, he published several books, including *Meditaciones para religiosos* ("Meditations for Religious"), 1982; *Reflexiones sobre la vida apostólica* ("Reflections on the Apostolic Life"), 1986; and *Reflexiones de esperanza* ("Reflections of Hope"), 1992. In 1986, he received permission to go to Germany to complete his doctorate in theology at Freiburg, and on returning to Argentina he taught and served as a spiritual director and confessor for the Society of Jesus in Córdoba. He was well known in the order for his expertise in Ignatian spirituality, the school of spirituality developed by Saint Ignatius Loyola.

Saint Ignatius's spiritual experiences during a year of prayer and contemplation at Manresa, Spain, in 1522-23 led to the development of his beloved Spiritual Exercises, which form the basis of one of the great spiritual schools in the history of the Church. Untold numbers of priests, religious, and laypeople have progressed through the Exercises over the centuries. Typically, qualified spiritual directors offer the Spiritual Exercises in closed sessions for a weekend, five days, eight days, or the full thirty days. The purpose is to use the heart, mind, and imagination to encounter Jesus in prayer, develop detachment from earthly things, and heighten discernment for the will of God in our lives, which will bring true freedom.

The first principle of the Exercises states:

> The goal of our life is to live with God forever. God who loves us, gave us life. Our own response of love allows God's life to flow into us without limit. All the things in this world are gifts of God, presented to us so that we can know God more easily and make a return of love more readily. As a result, we appreciate and use all these gifts of God insofar as they help us develop as loving persons.

By the time of his election as Pope Francis, Bergoglio was not only an expert in the Spiritual Exercises, he had also undergone the full Exercises twice.

The typical path for a Jesuit would have been to continue teaching and serving, but to his surprise, he was informed on May 20, 1992, that he been appointed by Blessed John Paul II as an auxiliary bishop

✠

"WITH MERCY CHOSEN"

An episcopal motto traditionally expresses the personality and the philosophy of a bishop. When Fr. Bergoglio was first ordained a bishop in 1992 he chose *"miserando atque eligendo"* ("with mercy chosen") as his motto. The phrase is taken from Venerable Bede's homily on Christ's call of Saint Matthew and is in the Office of Readings for the Feast of Saint Matthew, September 21:

Jesus saw a man called Matthew sitting at the tax office, and he said to him: Follow me. Jesus saw Matthew, not merely in the usual sense, but more significantly with his merciful understanding of men.

He saw the tax collector and, because he saw him through the eyes of mercy and chose him *[miserando atque eligendo]*, he said to him: *Follow me.* This following meant imitating the pattern of his life — not just walking after him. Saint John tells us: *Whoever says he abides in Christ ought to walk in the same way in which he walked.*

And he rose and followed him. There is no reason for surprise that the tax collector abandoned earthly wealth as soon as the Lord commanded him. Nor should one be amazed that neglecting his wealth, he joined a band of men whose leader had, on Matthew's assessment, no riches at all. Our Lord summoned Matthew by speaking to him in words. By an invisible, interior impulse flooding his mind with the light of grace, he instructed him to walk in his footsteps. In this way Matthew could understand that Christ, who was summoning him away from earthly possessions, had incorruptible treasures of heaven in his gift.

of Buenos Aires and the titular bishop of Auca. Pope John Paul had made the choice chiefly at the behest of Cardinal Antonio Quarracino, archbishop of Buenos Aires, who had been impressed by Bergoglio's intelligence and his reputation as a spiritual director. Bergoglio was ordained a bishop on June 27, 1992, and took as his episcopal motto, *"miserando atque eligendo"* ("with mercy chosen").

As an auxiliary bishop, he assisted the cardinal as the episcopal vicar to the Flores area of the archdiocese, and in 1993 was named vicar general, meaning that he was the chief administrator of the day-to-day needs of the archdiocese. He also made his first journey to Rome as a bishop when he attended the Ninth Ordinary Assembly of the Synod of Bishops in October 1994.

By then, he had become recognized for his presence among the poorest in the archdiocese, in the slums that were termed the *villas miserias* (villas of misery). He was additionally much in demand as a spiritual guide to the students and faculty of the Catholic University in Buenos Aires and as a confessor and counselor to the young people in the parishes, mainly in the Flores area.

Bishop Bergoglio was known as humble but insightful, and he kept the lowest profile among his episcopal colleagues in the archdiocese. It was thus a major surprise that on June 3, 1997, the announcement was made that he was to become the coadjutor archbishop of Buenos Aires. This meant that when the tenure of Cardinal Quarracino came to an end, Archbishop-designate Bergoglio would immediately accede to the see.

In November 1997, he returned to Rome to take part in the Special Assembly for America of the Synod of Bishops. The synod had as its purpose to study the state of the Church in the Americas under the title, "Encounter with the Living Jesus Christ: The Way to Conversion, Communion and Solidarity in America." In the synods of 1994 and 1997, he became more familiar with the dimensions of global Catholicism, and he also began to appreciate the complexity of the Vatican. Both perspectives were to deepen once he was an archbishop and a cardinal. As it was, Cardinal Quarracino died the next year, and Archbishop Bergoglio acceded to the see on Feb. 28, 1998.

He wasted no time leaving his mark on the archdiocese.

Chapter Eight

"JESUS IS THE DOOR"

———————⊕———————

"He who encounters Jesus Christ feels the impulse to witness him or to give witness of what he has encountered, and this is the Christian calling."

— CARDINAL JORGE MARIO BERGOGLIO, LECTURE, 2001

B uenos Aires has long been honored as the "Paris of South America." It is one of the most cosmopolitan, sophisticated, elegant, and alluring metropolises in the whole of the Western Hemisphere. The city of three million (about twelve million in the metropolitan area) ranks as arguably the most important city of Latin America, rivaled only by Mexico City and São Paulo. It cultivates a rich cafe culture, and the *porteños* savor *café con leche* and *medialuna* (a type of sweet roll), shop along the elegant Calle Florida, watch live tango or browse the antique market Feria de San Telmo on the Plaza Dorrego during the weekend, and enjoy leisurely strolls through the city's many parks, accompanied by the squawks of bright green parrots.

But there is another Buenos Aires. The official unemployment rate for the city is 15.2 percent, but it's estimated that a third of metropolitan Buenos Aires's residents lives below the poverty line, roughly 4.4 million people. Hunger, violence, and lack of medical care are common in the fourteen official slums (called *villas miserias*), shantytowns crowded around trains stations where perhaps as much as 7 percent of the city's population now resides.

This reality of beauty side by side with hardship is a feature of many major cities in Latin America, but it had a very personal meaning to Jorge Mario Bergolgio. He had grown up in Buenos Aires. He was a *porteño*. He had seen economic and social turmoil as a boy, a Jesuit candidate, a priest, and as auxiliary bishop. On February 28, 1998, he became the archbishop of Buenos Aires. Not only were these his people, they were now in his care. In short order, he revealed just how deeply and seriously he took his responsibility: In keeping with the lovely image of a bishop being wedded to his diocese, he referred to the archdiocese of Buenos Aires as an *esposa*, a spouse.

The Paris of the South

The origins of Buenos Aires go back to March 1536 when the Spanish adventurer Pedro de Mendoza, with 1,500 men, fulfilled the command of the Spanish Crown to establish a settlement along the Río de la Plata. The area was not rich in silver and gold as expected, but the settlers gave the tenuous foundation the reassuring name of *Puerto de Nuestra Señora Santa María de Buen Ayre* (Port of Our Lady of Fair Winds).

The settlement did not last long. The local tribes of Querandí Indians, tired of the Spanish and their many demands, refused to trade with them and eventually grew hostile and destroyed the weakened Spanish presence in the region.

Juan de Garay and three hundred settlers achieved a second and permanent foundation for Buenos Aires in 1580. Investigating the Pampa to the west, they discovered that the cattle and horses of Mendoza's settlement had survived and had been breeding, creating the opportunity for the domestication of both as well as the beginning of the remarkable gaucho culture of the Pampa.

For the next few centuries, Buenos Aires was a small city governed indifferently by the Spanish viceroy of Peru. The city was relatively isolated and faced challenges in its expansion because of the hostility of the Indians and the severe restrictions placed on trade by the Spanish colonial system. Even in these early days, though, the center of the city was the Plaza Mayor, what is today the Plaza de Mayo, site of the city's three most important buildings: the town hall, the governor's house, and the cathedral.

By the early eighteenth century, Buenos Aires was producing vast amounts of agricultural goods as well as dried beef and cattle hides. In 1776, finally recognizing the city's economic importance to the region, the Spanish Crown named Buenos Aires the capital of the new Viceroyalty of the Río de la Plata. The development of the city,

BUENOS AIRES

Buenos Aires had enjoyed a long tradition of devotion to the Blessed Mother, starting with its very name. In fact, Buenos Aires is named in honor of the Virgin of Bonaria (the Virgin of Fair Winds) who has been traditionally revered in the city of Cagliari, Italy, and was well known among sailors, especially those from certain parts of Spain. When Pedro de Mendoza established the settlement along the Río de la Plata in 1536, he named it in her honor on the occasion of the blessing of the expedition's chapel: *Puerto de Nuestra Señora Santa María de Buen Ayre* (Port of Our Lady Mary of Fair Winds).

In 1580, when Juan de Garay reestablished the Spanish presence, he called the new settlement *Ciudad de la Santísima Trinidad y Puerto de Santa María del Buen Aire* (City of the Most Holy Trinity and Port of Saint Mary of the Fair Winds). The name Buenos Aires came into popular use in the seventeenth century.

however, made it a target for the British, who attacked Buenos Aires in 1806 and 1807. They were defeated by local troops, and the victory gave the citizens of Buenos Aires the resolve to declare independence from Spain in 1810. They spent the next six years fighting to achieve freedom. In 1816, other provinces in the area joined them, and Buenos Aires was proclaimed the capital of the United Provinces of Río de la Plata. In 1880, it was named the federal capital of Argentina. In the prosperity that followed, the city's dazzling architecture took shape in grand houses, buildings, monuments, and churches. Buenos Aires earned its title of "Paris of South America" during this period.

As the largest city in the country, as the capital, and as home for much of the population, the great and often bloody events in the nation's modern history primarily unfolded here.

"Fr. Jorge"

The Diocese of Buenos Aires was founded officially on April 6, 1620, out of the Diocese of Paraguay. Its first bishop was a Carmelite,

Pedro Carranza Salinas. Pope Blessed Pius IX declared it an arch-diocese on March 5, 1866, and its first cardinal, Santiago Copello, received the red hat in 1935. He was the first Argentine cardinal and the first cardinal from Latin America.

When he assumed the leadership in 1998, Archbishop Bergoglio inherited a Catholic community of 2.5 million souls, 91.5 percent of the total population of the city. There were 3,800 priests, 850 men religious, 2,000 women religious, and 181 parishes. He was the first Jesuit to serve as archbishop, and from the start Bergoglio made it clear that his lifelong commitment to the poor and his emphasis on humility and pastoral service were not going to end with his new office.

The archbishop's residence was a lovely and grand home, but the new archbishop chose not to live there. Instead, he took a small apart-ment on the second floor of the curia building, next to the metro-politan cathedral in the downtown neighborhood of San Nicolás and near Plaza de Mayo. He declined a personal staff to do his cooking, preferring to fix his own meals. He was only getting started.

The story soon spread that the archbishop had been seen on the subway. At first disbelieved, the story persisted: the head of the arch-diocese was riding the subway dressed as a simple priest. It turned out to be true. Archbishop Bergoglio, having dispensed with a driver and limousine and feeling that a taxi was a ridiculous waste of money, instead took the *colectivo*, the city bus, and even more often the sub-way, usually Linea D. He wore his basic black clericals and read the newspaper or conversed comfortably with the average *porteños* making their own way to work. He kept this up as cardinal, too.

When people addressed him formally as His Excellency, he asked them instead to call him "Fr. Jorge." This continued even as cardinal.

Without pretension, like a humble parish priest, he was always there for his people. In 2001, he paid a visit to AIDS patients and washed and kissed their feet. He started drug-rehab efforts, focused on vocational programs, regularly visited terminal cancer patients, and baptized the children of the city's parishes. In moments of trag-edy and loss, he was there. In 2004, a fire in a nightclub in Buenos Aires killed 175 people and injured hundreds more, many of them teenagers. Hearing about the disaster in the middle of the night, the cardinal hastened to the site, arriving before many of the firemen and ambulances. He consoled the stricken survivors, asked one of his auxiliary bishops to provide ongoing pastoral care for the families, and criticized the local government for what many saw as both regulatory failure in licensing the club and an inadequate response.

According to an article in The Associated Press following Bergoglio's election to the papacy, the poor of Buenos Aires are proud of their *papa villero* (slum pope), noting that he often showed up in the most dangerous parts of the city unannounced to share in humble meals, drink mate from a common straw (mate is the Argentinian national drink brewed from the leaves of an evergreen tree), hear confessions, and celebrate Mass. "I . . . remember him going on long walks through our muddy streets or talking to our children," one woman said. Jaidr Flores, a young radio host who convinced the notoriously media-shy cardinal to appear on air, was amazed, upon going to the cardinal's office, to see his desk crowded with photos of volunteers and recovered drug addicts. "He truly cares for us," Flores said.

In an interview with Vatican Radio, seminarians Br. Ricardo Saenz and Br. Carlos Padilla provided additional insight into Cardinal Bergoglio's solicitude for the poorest in Buenos Aires. "In Buenos Aires," they said, "he founded a vicariate called 'Priests for the Favelas.'. . . So in our diocese he has a little structure of priests working just in the *favelas*. He himself would go there; he would cook for them on Christmas day — even as cardinal. He would go several times a year to these places. He knows very well all his three hundred priests in the diocese . . . these are the places he loves to be."

Bergoglio was especially concerned about the plight of single mothers and their children and was distressed when some priests refused to baptize children born out of wedlock. In 2012, he spoke bluntly about this, using one of his homilies to excoriate the presence in the Church of what he termed "clerical hypocrites," lamenting the fact that they had forgotten that Jesus Christ bathed lepers and ate with prostitutes. "In our ecclesiastical region," he declared, "there are priests who don't baptize the children of single mothers because they weren't conceived in the sanctity of marriage. These are today's hypocrites. Those who clericalize the Church. Those who separate the people of God from salvation. And this poor girl who, rather than returning the child to sender, had the courage to carry it into the world, must wander from parish to parish so that it's baptized!"

In a 2009 interview with *30 Days*, Cardinal Bergoglio said:

> The child has no responsibility for the marital state of its parents. And then, the baptism of children often becomes a new beginning for parents. Usually there is a little catechesis before baptism, about an hour, then a mystagogic catechesis during liturgy. Then, the priests and laity go to visit these families to continue with their post-baptismal pastoral. And it often happens that parents, who were not married in church, maybe ask to come before the altar to celebrate the sacrament of marriage.

He added a personal story:

> Just a few days ago I baptized seven children of a woman on her own, a poor widow, who works as a maid, and she had had them from two different men. I met her last year at the feast of San Cayetano. She'd said: "Father, I'm in mortal sin, I have seven children, and I've never had them baptized." It had happened because she had no money to bring the godparents from a distance, or to pay for the party, because she always had to work. . . . I suggested we meet, to talk about it.
>
> We spoke on the phone, she came to see me, told me that she could never find all the godparents and get them together. . . . In the end, I said, "Let's do everything with only two godparents, representing the others." They all came here, and after a little catechesis I baptized them in the chapel of the archbishopric. After the ceremony, we had a little refreshment. A Coca-Cola and sandwiches. She told me, "Father, I can't believe it, you make me feel important.". . . I replied, "But lady, where do I come in, it's Jesus who makes you important."

His choice of the apartment and his use of the bus were gestures of humility and service, but they had a specific grounding. As he said in 2004, after washing and kissing the feet of cancer patients, "This gesture is an invitation to the heart of every Christian, because we never lose if we imitate Jesus, if we . . . serve our suffering brothers."

✠

We never lose if we imitate Jesus, if we . . . serve our suffering brothers.

— CARDINAL JORGE MARIO BERGOGLIO

He used the occasion of his appointment as a cardinal to drive home the same point. Pope Blessed John Paul II appointed Archbishop Bergoglio to the College of Cardinals on February 21, 2001. When Bergoglio learned that Argentinians were planning to travel in large pilgrimages to Rome for the consistory, he issued a letter asking the faithful of Buenos Aires not to go. Instead, he requested that they use the money to feed the poor. He did the same when elected pope.

And then there was the matter of the cardinal's robes and vestments. He decided not to order new vestments, as was expected for a new cardinal, but had Cardinal Quarracino's old cardinal robes altered to fit him.

Matching his humility in service is what Cardinal Bergoglio often called "apostolic courage." In that sense, he was a prophetic voice as archbishop and cardinal and was unafraid to stand firm in defending the rights and dignity of the human person, speaking out against secularism and materialism and proclaiming the authentic teachings of the Church in Argentina and Latin America. Two incidents were revealing. The first came in the wake of Argentina's severe financial and economic crisis in 2001–02; the second in the face of the march toward secularism and relativism in the country.

Economic Crises

With the end of the junta in 1983, Argentina was at last able to hold democratic elections. The vote brought to power the Radical Party, which had the two mighty challenges of healing the nation and repairing the economy. They failed on the economic front, and battered by hyperinflation they were routed in the 1989 elections. The vote marked the return of the Perónist Party, headed by Carlos Menem, who pushed for privatization and policies designed to strengthen the peso. Inflation was brought under control, but a devastating recession swelled the ranks of the unemployed.

The Alliance Party, backed by the Radical Party, came to power under Fernando de la Rúa. Faced with crippling debt, he was forced to adopt austerity measures to prevent default by the country. The currency was further devalued and rumors of default caused massive panic and further devaluation. The middle class was devastated, and the plight of the poor grew even worse. To stop bank runs by terrified Argentinians, the government limited cash withdrawals.

In December 2001, angry Argentinians took to the streets, marching, rioting, and looting shops. More than twenty-seven people were killed and many feared that the country would sink once again into total chaos. President de la Rúa resigned and was followed by four presidents in eleven days. Next came a default that wiped out the savings of millions of people.

Throughout the crisis, Cardinal Bergoglio urged everyone in the country to avoid violence and cautioned against the many schemes that were being proposed, aware of the terrible impact they would have on the lives of average Argentinians, particularly the middle class and the poor. And he spoke out against the harsh treatment of workers whose only crime was protesting the financial incompetence of their leaders, contrasting the "poor people who are persecuted for demanding work, and rich people who are applauded for fleeing from justice."

The next year, he called for a spiritual renewal for the nation as a prerequisite for restoring its economic condition. As he said in a homily:

> To those who are now promising to fix all our problems, I say, "Go and fix yourself.". . . Have a change of heart. Get to confession, before you need it even more! The current crisis will not be improved by magicians from outside the country and nor will [improvement] come from the golden mouth of our politicians, so accustomed to making incredible promises.

In the wake of the financial and economic meltdown, Cardinal Bergoglio emerged as the only leader of national prominence with the slightest credibility. He was acknowledged for his compassion for the suffering of the Argentine people but also for his firm warnings about the impact of financial policies. His reference in a homily in 2002 about "magicians from outside the country" was also a manifestation of his worries regarding globalization, increasingly the cause of misery in Latin America. He warned that because of these economic policies, "Argentina looks ever more like a funeral procession where everyone wants to console the family but no one wants to carry the dead."

It was widely understood in Argentinian politics that any hopes for a bright future could be enhanced by a visit to see the archbishop of Buenos Aires, who was respected by leaders of every party. As for Bergoglio, whether as archbishop or cardinal, he remained always the same: unimpressed by the flattery of politicians, and speaking of the needs of the poor and the average Argentine.

As events proceeded, the elections of 2003 ended with the choice of President Néstor Kirchner. He enacted various policies in a quest to restore the economy. He was able to restructure Argentina's debt and used nationalization to spur economic growth.

Once again, Cardinal Bergoglio was not hesitant in speaking out that the policies could have a dire impact on the most vulnerable in Argentine society. As was his habit, he used the pulpit to make himself heard. His homily on the Ten Commandments and the beatitudes reminded Argentinians of the way of Jesus that teaches, "to trample upon the dignity of a woman, a man, a child, the elderly, is a grave sin that cries to heaven." As predicted, Argentina emerged out of its economic mire, but it endured high unemployment that still persists as well as suffering for the poor and the middle class.

Unhappy with the criticism, Kirchner made a less-than-veiled attack on the cardinal by suggesting, "Our God belongs to all, but watch out the devil also reaches everyone, those of us that wear pants and those that wear cassocks." He went on to declare that Cardinal Bergoglio was the "head of the opposition," an unsuccessful effort to

---

✠

Do you praise God. Do you praise God because he is so great as we do in the Mass? . . . Do you adore God? Are you stunned before this great God and adore him because he is the only God?

— CARDINAL JORGE MARIO BERGOGLIO, IN AN EWTN INTERVIEW

suggest Bergoglio had political motivations. As every major political figure of every stripe in the country sought to be publicly associated with the cardinal, it was a characterization generally dismissed as absurd posturing.

In 2005, Kirchner engaged in what was seen as an act of pettiness. Stung by the cardinal's criticism, he ended the almost two-century tradition of Argentine presidents commemorating May 25, Argentina's independence day, at a special Mass and *Te Deum* in the cathedral in Buenos Aires. Instead, he organized a celebration in a western province. Cardinal Bergoglio used his homily at the May 25 celebration the next year to assert, "Power is born of confidence, not with manipulation, intimidation, or with arrogance," and he decried "exhibitionism and loud announcements." The Kirchners, naturally, assailed the comments as a personal attack upon them.

What made the reaction so unfortunate was that Cardinal Bergoglio never made his criticisms personal. The relationship with the Kirchner government was hardly ever a happy one, but he had taken on governments before. Equally, the cardinal was pointing out that the Kirchners were engaging in propaganda and manipulation of the media, and in some cases even pushing toward censorship of the press. The Archdiocese of Buenos Aires, frustrated that the economic numbers the government was giving to the press were not consistent with its surveys and real-world experience — conspicuously in the area of unemployment and poverty — took to releasing its own statistics. While the Argentine media, captivated and intimidated by the charismatic Kirchners, regularly failed to report the accurate numbers, many global outlets and think tanks did rely on them, wanting numbers that reflected what was actually going on in the Argentinian economy.

Adding to the unhappiness at the *Casa Rosada* (the Pink House), the presidential palace on the Plaza de Mayo, was the election of Cardinal Bergoglio on November 9, 2005, to the post of president of the Argentina Episcopal Conference (the Bishops Conference) for the 2005-08 term; he was reelected for the 2008-11 term on November 11, 2008. The role positioned the cardinal to organize the conference so that it could speak to the key issues and proposals being advanced by the Kirchners.

In 2007, Néstor decided against running for reelection. This paved the way for the election of his wife, Cristina Fernández de Kirchner. Her husband had focused on economic matters, but Cristina's primary concerns included a radical agenda of secularization and progressive social policies.

There was one last chapter in Cardinal Bergoglio's dealings with Néstor Kirchner. Néstor died in October 2010, and Cardinal Bergoglio expressed his sadness at the passing and offered to celebrate a Mass in his memory. Speaking from the same pulpit in the metropolitan cathedral from which he had castigated the policies of the government, Cardinal Bergoglio said:

> The people should let go of any antagonism they have when faced with the death of the man who was anointed by the people to lead the country, and the whole country should pray for him. . . .
>
> It would be a sign of ingratitude if this nation's people did not come together in prayer for this man who took up, heart and soul, the task of uniting the people who had asked him to lead them.

Social Crises

Buoyed by the gradually improving economy, Cristina Kirchner advanced her social agenda and her efforts to further tighten control over much of the Argentinian press. There was thus little respite for the Church, which continued to find itself confronting the government on several points, the most significant being abortion and same-sex marriage.

A supporter of the radical progressive social agenda being promoted in other Latin America countries as well as in Europe and North America, Cristina had initially run as a pro-life candidate. She changed course abruptly once in power. But there were significant legislative difficulties involved in changing Argentina's laws on abortion — it is illegal in the constitution, although there are certain exemptions in the penal code, such as for medical conditions, deformed fetuses, and situations where the mother is mentally ill or mentally challenged.

Christina used her allies in the National Congress to open alternative regulatory channels. In 2007, the Chamber of Deputies' Public

Health and Assistance Committee and the Penal Legislation Committee advanced a bill that took existing exemptions in the criminal code for penalties for abortion and created a "protocol" for expanded exemptions. The exemptions would include conditions such as "health risk," significantly expanding the availability of abortion because of the plasticity of the language. For example, it was noted by pro-life forces that under such a protocol, "health" could be extended to include the psychological state of the mother or even her social situation. This bill has since been making its way through the Argentine legislature. In March 2012, the Supreme Court of Argentina ruled that abortion in case of rape or a threat to a woman's life is legal and that an affidavit attesting to being raped would be sufficient for a legal abortion to take place.

Cardinal Bergoglio, as archbishop of Buenos Aires and as head of the Argentinian Episcopal Conference, had been outspoken in his opposition to these backdoor efforts to bring abortion to Argentina. In 2012, as the Supreme Court pushed ahead with its decision, Cardinal Bergoglio said: "Abortion is never a solution. We listen, support and [offer] understanding from our place to save two lives: respect the human being small and helpless, they can take steps to preserve your life, allow birth, and then be creative in the search for ways to bring it to its full development."

Prior to this, Cardinal Bergoglio helped to organize a document on the concerns, challenges, and aspirations of the Church in Latin America during the 2007 Fifth General Conference of the Latin American and Caribbean Bishops' Conferences held in Aparecida, Brazil. The concluding document included a powerful restatement on the Church's commitment to life and also to family. It said:

> Today we stand before new challenges that call us to be the voice of the voiceless. The child growing in its mother's womb and people who are in their declining years are a claim for dignified life that cries out to heaven and that cannot but make us shudder. The liberalization and routinization of abortion practices are abominable crimes, just as are euthanasia, genetic and embryonic manipulation, unethical medical testing, capital punishment, and so many other ways of assaulting the dignity and life of the

✠

If we want to maintain a solid and inviolable basis for human rights, we absolutely must recognize that human life must always be defended from the very moment of conception.

— CARDINAL JORGE MARIO BERGOGLIO

human being. If we want to maintain a solid and inviolable basis for human rights, we absolutely must recognize that human life must always be defended from the very moment of conception. Otherwise, the circumstances and conveniences of the powerful will always find excuses for abusing persons.

Kirchner has also tackled the divisive issue of same-sex marriage. Due, in part, to her aggressive advocacy of a bill to legalize same-sex marriage, on July 22, 2010, Argentina became the first Latin American country to allow same-sex marriage.

Cardinal Bergoglio led a spirited effort to prevent the new law. He spoke out publicly, urged Catholics to work and pray for the defeat of the legislation, and, according to Rorate Caeli, a Catholic blog, he wrote a letter to the Carmelite nuns of the Archdiocese of Buenos Aires on June 22, 2010, that said, in part:

The identity of the family, and its survival, are in jeopardy here: father, mother, and children. . . . A clear rejection of the law of God, engraved in our hearts, is in jeopardy. . . .

Here, the envy of the devil, through which sin entered the world, is also present, and deceitfully intends to destroy the image of God: man and woman, who receive the mandate to grow, multiply, and conquer the earth.

Let us not be naive: it is not a simple political struggle; it is an intention [which is] destructive of the plan of God. It is not a mere legislative project (this is a mere instrument), but rather a "move" of the Father of Lies who wishes to confuse and deceive the children of God.

Kirchner responded with an all-out media campaign in which she accused the cardinal of having a mind trapped in the Middle Ages. In the end, the bishops' conference could not prevent the bill from passing. It was a lesson, though, in ruthless politics.

Tied intimately to the slow advance of the culture of death was another concern for Cardinal Bergoglio: the defense, promotion, and renewal of Catholic life and practice.

Cultural Crisis

It was well known in Buenos Aires that Cardinal Bergoglio rarely granted interviews to the media. When he spoke about issues, he usually did so through homilies, delivered with fire at the cathedral. In fact, from 1998 to his appointment as cardinal in 2001, he gave only one interview. It was not with a major newspaper or television network, but with a small parish news bulletin, *Estrellita de Belen* (Little Star of Bethlehem). The interviewer asked about Catholic identity, but Bergoglio stopped the questioner when he mentioned that Argentina was a majority Catholic country. The cardinal disagreed and said flatly that the levels of corruption, toxic messages in the media, and social inequalities could not possibly describe a Catholic country.

His observation underscored a point that is central to his work: the need to nurture authentic Catholic culture as an essential element in the defense of the dignity of the human person and as a key to building a truly just society. In this regard, he has never been afraid to address forcefully the weaknesses in Argentine culture. Bergoglio has been described as shy and rather retiring before crowds, but his preaching is both commanding and passionate. In 2010, he delivered a homily during a Mass at the Constitution train station that narrowed in on the visceral image of Buenos Aires as a "meat grinder" because of its treatment of human beings trapped in prostitution, human trafficking, and horrific labor conditions.

> In this city there are many slaves! I said this last year and I repeat it . . . sweatshops . . . trafficking of girls in prostitution . . . for many our city is a meat grinder because it shatters their lives and breaks the will. The night before last, a poor girl was taken out of a brothel and had to be hospitalized in intensive care at one of our hospitals because to break her will they gave her psychotropics,

and she entered a coma. . . . That happens in this city! This city makes these great mafia lords very elegant! They may eat in Puerto Madero restaurants, but their money is stained with blood. . . . They are the enslavers!

And when we read the stories of ancient civilizations, in pagan cults human sacrifices were made, people were killed, and we were horrified. . . . In this city are made human sacrifices that kill the dignity of these men and women, these boys and girls subjected to trafficking and slavery. We cannot stay quiet. This city is full of men and women, boys and girls beaten by the wayside, beaten by the organization or organizations that are corrupting, removing the will, even destroying them with drugs. And then they are left lying by the roadside.

He also spoke of a culture in Buenos Aires that discards those who are seen as inefficient or no longer functional. He referred to this as a "hidden euthanasia" that seeks to dispose of the elderly even though they represent an important seat of wisdom. As he later observed to the College of Cardinals after his election as Pope Francis:

Old age is — as I like to say — the seat of life's wisdom. The old have acquired the wisdom that comes from having journeyed through life, like the old man Simeon, the old prophetess Anna in the Temple. And that wisdom enabled them to recognize Jesus. Let us pass on this wisdom to the young: like good wine that improves with age, let us give life's wisdom to the young. I am reminded of a German poet who said of old age: *Es is ruhig, das Alter, und fromm*: it is a time of tranquility and prayer. And also a time to pass on this wisdom to the young.

His solution to this crisis in culture was to summon all the Catholics of Argentina — to summon the Church — to proclaim Jesus Christ. He made this clear in his remarkable letter to the Catholics of the Archdiocese of Buenos Aires on October 1, 2012, the feast of Saint Thérèse of the Child Jesus, to mark the Year of Faith.

One of the most powerful impressions in recent decades has been the experience of finding closed doors. Growing insecurity has been leading people, little by little, to lock the doors, to install safety devices and security cameras, to distrust the stranger who calls at the door. Nevertheless, in some neighborhoods there still are doors that are open.

The closed door is a perfect symbol of today's world. It is something more than a simple sociological fact; it is an existential reality that characterizes a lifestyle, a way to stop confronting reality, dealing with others, and facing the future. The closed door of my house, which is the intimate place of my dreams, my hopes and sufferings, and also of my joys, is closed to others.

And this is not just about my material house; this is true also of the enclosed area of my life, my heart. Fewer and fewer people can cross this threshold. The security of some shuttered doors guards the insecurity of a life that is becoming more fragile and less susceptible to the risks of life and to the love of others. The image of an open door has always been the symbol of light, friendship, joy, freedom, confidence. How we need to recover these things! The closed door harms us, paralyzes us, separates us. . . .

Someone goes through the door of faith, this threshold is crossed, when the Word of God is proclaimed and the heart allows itself to be molded by the grace that transforms it. A grace that bears a specific name, and this name is Jesus. Jesus is the door (see Jn 10:9). He, and he alone, is and always will be the door. No one goes to the Father except through him (Jn 14:6). If there is no Christ, there is no way to God. As a door he opens up for us the way to God, and as the Good Shepherd he is the only One who cares for us at the cost of his own life.

Jesus is the door and calls at our door so that we will let him cross the threshold of our life. "Be not afraid . . . open the doors to Christ," Blessed John Paul II told us at the beginning of his pontificate. Open the doors of the heart as the disciples did in Emmaus, asking the Lord to remain *with us so that we can go through the doors of faith*: the same Lord leads us to understand the reasons why we believe, *so as then to go out and proclaim him*. Faith involves deciding to be with the Lord so as to live with him and to share him with our brethren.

In the interviews that he gave in the time before his election, he picked up on the image of the open door and the call to share Christ. Speaking with *Vatican Insider* magazine in February 2012, the cardinal discussed what that meant specifically in Argentina and Buenos Aires:

We seek to make contact with families that are not involved in the parish. Instead of just being a Church that welcomes and receives, we try to be a Church that comes out of itself and goes to the men and women who do not participate in parish life, do not know much about it, and are indifferent toward it.

We organize missions in public squares where many people usually gather: we pray, we celebrate Mass, we offer baptism which we administer after a brief preparation. This is the style of the parishes and the diocese itself. Other than this, we also try to reach out to people who are far away, via digital means, the Web, and brief messaging.

Cardinal Bergoglio's approach to the crisis in culture has been both pastoral and passionate. On Palm Sunday 2008, he told a packed cathedral in Buenos Aires: "Today the place for Christ is the street; the place for the Christian is the street. The Lord wants us like him: with an open heart, roaming the streets of Buenos Aires. He wants us walking the streets of Buenos Aires and carrying his message!"

An Archbishop and His Priests

The metropolitan cathedral in Buenos Aries is a magnificent neo-classical church with a Baroque and Rococo interior that has been rebuilt several times over the centuries. Its facade has twelve columns symbolizing the Twelve Apostles, its main altar, a Rococo masterpiece, is silver-plated, and the cathedral's exceptional life-size statue of Christ is carved out of native *caroh* wood. From 1998 until early in 2013, it was also the cathedral of Cardinal Bergoglio, where he proclaimed the truths of the Catholic faith and where he performed most of the ordinations over the course of those years.

As a bishop, of course, he was a father to his priests, but he demanded that they share in his own love for the poor and the defenseless. He asked nothing of them, however, that he was not willing to do himself. In an interview with *30 Days* in 2001, he said:

I have told my priests: "Do everything you should, you know your duties as ministers, take your responsibilities and then leave the door open." Our sociologists of religion tell us that the influence of a parish has a radius of six hundred meters. In Buenos

Aires there are about two thousand meters between one parish and the next. So I then told the priests: "If you can, rent a garage and, if you find some willing layman, let him go there! Let him be with those people a bit, do a little catechesis, and even give Communion if they ask him."

A parish priest said to me: "But Father, if we do this the people then won't come to church." "But why?" I asked him: "Do they come to Mass now?" "No," he answered. And so! Coming out of oneself is also coming out from the fenced garden of one's own convictions, considered irremovable, if they risk becoming an obstacle, if they close the horizon that is also of God.

His priests, in turn, praised the cardinal as a fatherly and supportive presence for them. Every priest reportedly received his private cell-phone number with permission to call when in need of help or guidance. He was so heavily involved in the life of the seminary and the formation of seminarians that young priests there are known as "the Bergoglio generation." When any of his priests were in personal crisis, he was there, and when they were dying, he made it a point to sit next to their deathbeds for hours at a time, reading to them and praying with them.

An able manager as well, he modernized the administration of the archdiocese and was one of the first advocates in Latin America for the use of the Internet and social media as tools of the Faith.

His own daily routines were well known to his priests and served as an example in their own priestly lives. Fr. Guillermo Marcó, Cardinal Bergoglio's spokesman from 1998 to 2006, told NBC Latino, that the cardinal's daily routine was well established:

Cardinal Bergoglio would wake up around 4:30 or 5:00 a.m. and then conduct his morning prayers. By 7:00 a.m., after having a light breakfast, he would read the papers. Then, until 8:00 a.m., he would remain close to a landline telephone. Every priest in town knew that phone's number, and every one of them knew that they could call every morning between 7:00 and 8:00 if they had any problem. The cardinal himself would pick up the phone. Not any secretary, not any clerical adjutant, but Archbishop Bergoglio. He would listen to their complaints and their requests, and he would jot down his observations in a small pocketbook with small, almost microscopic handwriting. Only then would he walk down to his office, just a few steps away.

Fr. Marcó added that the cardinal avoided lavish lunches and dinners, preferring a relaxed lunch and an apple and a cup of tea for dinner. He had a fondness for long walks, listened to classical music and opera, and enjoyed great literature. His favorite authors were the Argentinians Jorge Luis Borges and Leopoldo Marechal, and, as we have seen, the Russian novelist Dostoyevsky.

The stories of his humility and utter lack of pretension were so commonplace that the people of the archdiocese eventually ceased being amazed by them. His ministry touched countless *porteños* as well as his small, gentle acts of kindness. Some wished to return the favor. One that had greater significance than was realized at the time

SAN LORENZO DE ALMAGRO

From his childhood, Pope Francis has been a fan of the *fútbol* (soccer) team San Lorenzo de Almagro that was founded by a priest with the hope of keeping young men off the streets and away from violence and gangs. The team hails from the central Buenos Aires neighborhood of Almagro, and their fans take as their symbol the crow (*cuervo*). He said many times that he tried to go to matches as often as possible and is officially listed as member 88,235.

In 2008, Cardinal Bergoglio offered to say Mass for the team's one-hundredth anniversary. On May 24, 2011, he celebrated Mass on the feast of *María Auxiliadora* (Mary Auxiliatrix) in the chapel of San Lorenzo's stadium. He said: "Keep María Auxiliadora in San Lorenzo because she is our mother, as San Lorenzo was born in San Antonio's Church under the protection of the Virgin. I feel a great joy to celebrate Mass looking through the windows of the Chapel of San Lorenzo stadium."

Upon the pope's election, the team issued a statement of happiness and pride.

involved a pair of shoes. Before he headed to Rome for the conclave to elect the successor to Pope Benedict XVI, Cardinal Bergoglio had a conversation with friends about the deplorable condition of his shoes. They asked him to accept a new pair that he could wear into the august setting of the Vatican and the Sistine Chapel. He reluctantly agreed, and after his election as Francis, he chose not to wear the papal red shoes. Instead, he kept the new black shoes that had been given him so generously by friends.

The Cardinal from Argentina

The elevation to the cardinalate meant that Bergoglio would now be obligated to go more often to Rome and to take on more international travel beyond that. He was never fond of travel and disliked being away from Buenos Aires for long stretches of time. When he went to Rome, he normally took a small room at the austere Casa del Clero and carried his own luggage.

Still, the position brought new responsibilities because every cardinal serves as a member of various offices in the Roman Curia to advise and assist in the work of the Holy See. In the twelve years from the time of his appointment, he went to Rome several times a year, working as a member of the Congregations for Divine Worship and the Discipline of the Sacraments, for the Clergy, for the Institutes of Consecrated Life and the Societies of Apostolic Life, and of the Pontifical Council for the Family.

In addition, he went to Rome to take part in the various synods of bishops, the gatherings of bishops from around the world to discuss important issues facing the Church. In October 2001, he was asked suddenly to take over as relator (or leader) of a synod on the role of the bishop when Cardinal Edward Egan of New York was forced to stay home after the September 11 attacks. Cardinal Bergoglio proved remarkably popular and earned a considerable reputation for his efficient but fraternal approach to the deliberations.

He was back in Rome in April 2005 for the funeral of Pope John Paul II and then the conclave to elect his successor. Significantly, his name began appearing on the various lists of *papabili* with high praise coming from many quarters for the skill of his governance of Buenos

Aires and for his spiritual and intellectual gifts. He was sixty-eight, a suitable age, and many believed that the time had come for a pontiff from beyond the boundaries of Europe.

The conclave itself ended with the election of Cardinal Joseph Ratzinger as Pope Benedict XVI, and it was widely reported that Cardinal Bergoglio had supported his candidacy and was delighted with the choice. In the next months, stories also circulated that Cardinal Bergoglio had received a substantial number of votes in the conclave. The truth of that remains a mystery because of the secrecy imposed by conclave rules. What was absolutely certain, however, was that Cardinal Bergoglio was ranked among the most respected Church leaders in all of Latin America and was well known among his fellow cardinals.

His profile increased even further among the Latin American bishops during the Fifth General Conference of the Latin American Episcopate in May 2007. At the end of the conference, he was elected to head the commission of bishops charged with writing the all-important final report that would be used to chart the course for Latin America in the coming years. Once more he proved his gifts as a consensus builder able to work in a spirit of collaboration. The final document was a blueprint for the future, and Cardinal Bergoglio's influence is manifest in its pages:

> In Latin America and the Caribbean, at a time when many of our peoples are preparing to celebrate the bicentenary of their independence, we find ourselves facing the challenge of revitalizing our way of being Catholic and our personal options for the Lord, so that Christian faith may become more deeply rooted in the heart of Latin American individuals and peoples as a founding event and living encounter with Christ.
>
> He reveals himself as newness of life and mission in all dimensions of personal and social existence. This requires, on the basis of our Catholic identity, a much more missionary evangelization, in dialogue with all Christians and at the service of all people.

In February 2012 and again in November 2012, the cardinal was in Rome for the consistories of cardinals that welcomed new members to the College of Cardinals. And then, like the rest of the Church, he was surprised by the news on February 11 that Pope Benedict XVI would resign. The level of media interest in Bergoglio was now rather different from 2005. While deeply respected by his fellow cardinals, the world's press, in large measure, largely ignored him because he was now seventy-six years old and conventional wisdom said the cardinals would be looking for someone much younger. To be sure, quiet words were said about his potential viability, but the focus was always elsewhere.

Based upon small clues that have emerged here and there, he arrived in the conclave with considerable support. That support grew, and he

---

COAT OF ARMS

At the time he was named a bishop in 1992, Bishop Bergoglio was invited to design a coat of arms that traditionally serves as a visual statement of the philosophy and sensibilities of a bishop. While they are free to change their coat of arms, most bishops keep them throughout their ecclesiastical careers. The coat of arms taken by Pope Francis is, in fact, based on the one he designed when he was first made a bishop.

The papal coat of arms has a shield with a blue background. Blue is the traditional color of the Blessed Mother. Dominating the blue field is the traditional symbol of the Society of Jesus, the Jesuits, a flaming gold sun with the three nails of the Crucifixion beneath the letters "IHS" signifying Jesus's name, all surmounted by a cross. It was chosen because Pope Francis is a member of the Jesuits.

To the lower left is a solid gold five-pointed star, which symbolizes the Blessed Mother, and a nard flower, in gold, one of the ancient symbols of Saint Joseph. Taken together, the three symbols offer an image of the Holy Family: Jesus, Mary, and Joseph.

The crest is surmounted by the traditional symbols of the papacy, the crossed keys, silver and gold, tied together by a red chord, and a mitre that was first adopted by Pope Benedict XVI in 2005. His episcopal motto in Latin is *Miserando atque eligendo*, which means "with mercy chosen," and is from Bede's Homily 21, on the call of Saint Matthew.

was elected on the fifth ballot of the second day. It was widely reported that he received far more votes than the seventy-seven required. At the moment of his election, his close friend, Brazilian Cardinal Claudio Hummes, who was seated next to him, reminded him not to forget the poor.

On February 19, just before he left for Rome to say farewell to Pope Benedict and then to take part in the conclave, Cardinal Bergoglio published what turned out to be his final letter as archbishop of Buenos Aries, this one for Lent. He wrote:

OUR LADY OF LUJÁN

The Patroness of Argentina, Paraguay, and Uruguay, Our Lady of Luján is revered throughout Argentina. Devotion to Mary under this title began when a seventeenth-century Portuguese settler, intent on reviving the weak faith of the people, had a friend bring an icon of Mary into the country from Brazil. The caravan carrying the treasure paused near Buenos Aires on its way to its final destination, Cordova, but the horses pulling the wagon with the icon refused to go forward. Every attempt to prod them failed, but when the icon was removed, the animals willingly resumed the journey. The icon ultimately found its way to the Sanctuary of Luján, where it is still on display, and many miracles have been attributed to Mary's intercession there. In 1930, Pope Pius XI gave the sanctuary — a cathedral constructed in the early twentieth century — the title of basilica. Pope John Paul II visited in 1982 and bestowed the Golden Rose, a delicate blossom rendered in gold and a special papal honor reserved for nations, cities, basilicas, or shrines.

Each year, in October, tens of thousands of pilgrims take part in the nearly fifty-mile walk from Buenos Aires to Luján, a pilgrimage that has included Cardinal Bergoglio. The chalice Argentina gave Pope Francis in honor of his election to the papacy incorporates into the design an image of Our Lady of Luján.

Little by little we become accustomed to hearing and seeing, through the mass media, the dark chronicle of contemporary society, presented with an almost perverse joy, and also we become desensitized to touching it and feeling it all around us, even in our own flesh. Drama plays out on the streets, in our neighborhoods, in our homes and — why not? — even in our own hearts. We live alongside a violence that kills, that destroys families, that sparks wars and conflicts in so many countries of the world. We live with envy, hatred, slander, the mundane in our heart.

The suffering of the innocent and peaceable buffets us non-stop; the contempt for the rights of the most fragile of people and nations is not so distant from us; the tyrannical rule of money with its demonic effects, such as drugs, corruption, trafficking in people — even children — along with misery, both material and moral, are the coin of the realm today. The destruction of dignified work, painful emigrations and the lack of a future also join in this heartbreaking symphony.

Our errors and sins as Church are not beyond this analysis. Rationalizing selfishness does not diminish it, lack of ethical values within a society metastasizes in our families, in the environment of our neighborhoods, towns and cities, this lack of ethical values testifies to our limitations, to our weaknesses and to our incapacity to transform this innumerable list of destructive realities.

The trap of powerlessness makes us wonder: Does it make sense to try to change all this? Can we do anything against this? Is it worthwhile to try, if the world continues its carnival merriment, disguising all this tragedy for a little while? But, when the mask falls, the truth appears and, although to many it may sound anachronistic to say so, once again sin becomes apparent, sin that wounds our very flesh with all its destructive force, twisting the destinies of the world and of the history.

Lent is presented to us as a shout of truth and certain hope that comes to us to say, "Yes, it is possible to not slap on makeup, and not draw plastic smiles as if nothing happened." Yes, it is possible that all is made new and different because God remains "rich in kindness and mercy, always willing to forgive," and he encourages us to begin anew time and again. Today, again, we are invited to undertake a Paschal road toward Life, a path that includes the Cross and resignation; a path that will be uncomfortable but not fruitless. We are invited to admit that something inside us is not going well (in society or in the Church), to change, to turn around, to be converted.

Chapter Nine

"GRACE ALWAYS COMES FIRST"

---✠---

Let us not yield to pessimism or discouragement: let us be quite certain that the Holy Spirit bestows upon the Church, with his powerful breath, the courage to persevere.

— POPE FRANCIS,
ADDRESS TO THE CARDINALS, MARCH 15, 2013

The election of Cardinal Jorge Mario Bergoglio, archbishop of Buenos Aires, as Pope Francis was unexpected. As has been noted, Pope Francis was a pope of many firsts at the time of his selection by the College of Cardinals — including the first pope from Latin America, the first Jesuit, and the first from the Southern Hemisphere.

The election has ramifications for the Church and for the world that will be playing out for years to come, but several points are certain.

For starters, based on the experience of the Church in Argentina, Catholics can expect Pope Francis to be humble and pastoral, but also ardent in his preaching and teaching.

Further, the choice has electrified the entire Church in Latin America and has, moreover, proven the source of intense excitement across those areas where the Church is growing rapidly — for example, in Africa and Asia.

At the same time, the cardinals' choice reveals that a current of reform — the *need* for reform — runs within the College of Cardinals and it led to Francis. He will help the Vatican government and offices to be truly at the service of the Petrine ministry so that the pope can better serve the Church.

Finally, Pope Francis will use gestures — such as when he paid his hotel bill after his election, or took the bus back to the residence

— to make key points about ecclesiastical pride and vanity. In this he is demonstrating simplicity-with-a-purpose: to clear away everything else so that the Church can proclaim Jesus Christ to the world.

Chapter Three provided a basic assessment of the chief issues that were on the minds of the cardinals as they prepared for the conclave. Based on those, it is possible to appreciate the enormity of the task that lies ahead for Pope Francis. Looking at the future, the Church faces three key areas of challenge:

- Modernity and the New Evangelization
- Global Catholicism
- Reform and Renewal

Modernity and the New Evangelization

In their message at the end of the Synod of Bishops on the New Evangelization in October 2012, the bishops wrote:

> Everywhere indeed we feel the need to revive a faith that risks eclipse in cultural contexts that hinders its taking root in persons and its presence in society, the clarity of its content and the coherence of its fruits. The changed social, cultural, economic, civil, and religious scenarios call us to something new: to live our communitarian experience of faith in a renewed way and to proclaim it through an evangelization that is "*new in its ardor, in its methods, in its expressions*," as John Paul II said. . . .
>
> Benedict XVI recalled that it is an evangelization that is directed "principally at those who, though baptized, have drifted away from the Church and live without reference to the Christian life . . . to help these people encounter the Lord, who alone fills our existence with deep meaning and peace; and to favor the rediscovery of the faith, that source of grace which brings joy and hope to personal, family and social life" (*Homily for the Eucharistic celebration for the solemn inauguration of the* XIII *Ordinary General Assembly of the Synod of Bishops*, Rome, October 7, 2012).

This succinct explanation of the task of the New Evangelization and its dimensions applies to every corner of the Church, not just the developed world where there is understandably a greater sense of immediacy.

Unsurprisingly, Europe and North America are considered the front lines of the effort. Europe still claims a quarter of the world's Catholic population (about 283 million) and though this might suggest that Catholicism on the Continent is holding steady, serious questions remain about the Faith's long-term sustainability there as the population ages and struggles with the crises of negative birthrates, abortion, euthanasia, and anti-family secularism.

Causes for the decline in the birthrate in the developed world are ample and obvious: the embrace of materialism, the cancerous presence of abortion and contraception, the decline of marriage, the failure of couples to want to have children or to severely limit the number. Most European countries have low or even negative growth rates. A replacement total birthrate (fertility rate) to maintain a stable population is 2.1 births per woman. In the United Kingdom, the rate is 1.91, in Germany the rate is 1.41, and in Italy it is 1.4 (source: 2012 CIA World Factbook). Worse, if the impact of immigrant families is removed, Europe's actual population would be shrinking.

Russia has a birthrate of 1.61, compounded by widespread problems of alcoholism, economic and social despair, and estimates are that annually 1.6 million Russian women have abortions while only 1.5 million gave birth. The Muslim population of Russia, meanwhile, is projected to increase as the rest of the Russian population declines; currently, there are approximately twenty million Muslims in Russia out of a population of almost 150 million.

Europe's sclerotic growth rates are more and more mirrored in North America. Canada has the lowest birthrate in the Americas and the United States is currently suffering from its lowest birthrate on record (2.06). The same problems of an aging population will emerge in the next decades as the baby-boom generation moves into its twilight years. Still, 22 percent of the total population in the United States is Catholic (essentially unchanged from fifty years ago), most due to heavy increases in the Latino population.

Paired with the collapse in birthrates are the slow erosion of Christian identity and even any sense of religious belief at all. In Great Britain, for example, the pace of this social fragmentation and secular transformation is astonishing. In December 2012, the British Office for National Statistics (ONS) published details of the 2011 census for England and Wales that revealed a decline in the number of those professing Christianity. In 2001, 72 percent of the population listed their religious affiliation as Christian. That number had declined, in only a decade, to 59 percent. At the same time, those who said they had "no religion" had risen by more than six million to about fourteen million in the same decade.

The same report revealed that in 2011, for the first time in the history of the census in England and Wales, a majority of the population was unmarried. The percentage of those married had fallen from 51 percent to 47 percent, with a couple's decision to cohabit given as the most common reason not to marry.

The decline of marriage, the societywide prevalence of divorce, the rise of human trafficking, the massive sea change underway in the area of gender identity, in particular the movement toward so-called same-sex marriage, all these and more point to a serious misunderstanding not only of Church teaching, but also of human anthropology about sexuality.

Cardinal Bergoglio, of course, has been a champion of the family in Argentina and across all of Latin America, resisting the legalization of abortion and same-sex marriage. His homilies have focused not only on strengthening the family, but also on drawing attention to the plight of women and children. In a 2011 homily during a Mass for victims of human trafficking, he said:

> In this city, there are many girls who stop playing with dolls to enter the dump of a brothel because they were kidnapped, sold, and trafficked. Today, we've come to pray for the victims of human trafficking, slave-labor trafficking, sexual trafficking for prostitution. . . . Contrary to what we're taught in school, slavery has not been abolished.
>
> You know what that is? A fairy tale! In this city, slavery is the order of the day in various forms, in this city workers are exploited in sweatshops and, if they're immigrants, they have no way out. In this city, there are kids who've lived on the streets for years. I don't know if the number is more or less, but there are

many, and the city failed and continues to fail in any attempt to free them from this structural slavery of homelessness.

In this city, women and girls are kidnapped and subjected to the use and abuse of their body; they are destroyed in their dignity. The human flesh that Jesus assumed and for which he died is worth less than the flesh of a house pet. We take better care of a dog than these slaves who we kick, who we destroy. I spent a couple of hours with the mother of Marita Verón, who was kidnapped by traffickers and sent to work in brothels. They managed to free 129 other girls, but her daughter still hasn't been found yet.

The Church's teaching about marriage, family life, the single life, cohabitation, and similar issues are all part of the content of the New Evangelization as the Synod of Bishops on the New Evangelization made clear:

> Established by the Sacrament of Matrimony, the Christian family as the domestic Church is the locus and first agent in the giving of life and love, the transmission of faith and the formation of the human person according to the values of the Gospel. . . .
>
> At the same time, the New Evangelization should strive to address significant pastoral problems around marriage, the case of divorced and remarried, the situation of their children, the fate of abandoned spouses, the couples who live together without marriage, and the trend in society to redefine marriage.
>
> The Church, with maternal care and evangelical spirit, should seek appropriate responses for these situations as an important aspect of the New Evangelization.
>
> Every pastoral plan of evangelization should also include a respectful invitation to all those who live alone, to experience God in the family of the Church.
>
> It is necessary to educate people in how to live human sexuality according to Christian anthropology, both before marriage as well as in marriage itself.

As we have seen, many other issues beyond sexuality — secularism, materialism, and atheism, for example — challenge the Church in these post-Christian, postmodern times. Can these trends be reversed? Is it too late?

Pope Francis arrives at the papacy at a time of crisis. He inherits from Pope Benedict a project of evangelization with a solid foundation, but it is still in its infancy. The Pontifical Council for Promoting the New Evangelization got underway in 2010, but the Synod of Bishops on the New Evangelization took place only very recently, in October 2012.

Pope Francis, picking up where Pope Benedict left off, has already begun to chart a course forward with his firm adherence to orthodoxy matched by a committed, self-sacrificing love for and compassion toward all people, especially the poor and broken. These are critical ingredients if the New Evangelization is to gain ground.

Practically speaking, meeting the challenges of modernity must include the essential dialogue between faith and reason. As the bishops said at the 2012 synod:

> The dialogue between science and faith is a vital field in the New Evangelization. On the one hand, this dialogue requires the openness of reason to the mystery which transcends it and an awareness of the fundamental limits of scientific knowledge. On the other hand, it also requires a faith that is open to reason and to the results of scientific research.

Closely allied to this dialogue is the call to reach out to those who have no religious affiliation or are even atheists. One innovative initiative in this regard is the so-called Courtyard of the Gentiles, gatherings in various cities between believers and nonbelievers organized by the Pontifical Council for Culture under the multilingual cardinal and philosopher Gianfranco Ravasi. Bergoglio recommended an even simpler approach when he told his priests to get out from behind their fences and engage people — maybe rent a garage and "do a little catechesis."

Reaching out to the world also includes the use of social media — every means at our disposal to connect with the great "digital continent," as Pope Benedict called it. Pope Francis has already plunged ahead in this regard, using technology and social media for evangelization and communication as part of his wider program of modernization for the Church in Buenos Aires. As pope, of course, he now assumes the papal Twitter account, with the handle, @pontifex.

✠

---

*We need to avoid the spiritual sickness of a Church that is wrapped
up in its own world: when a Church becomes like this, it grows sick.*

— CARDINAL BERGOGLIO

Pope Francis will press ahead with the New Evangelization using
the work of the synod as his blueprint. As we will see, he is likely to
advance a *global* call to the New Evangelization — beyond the needs
of the developed world — reflecting the worldwide growth of secularism and the impact of the phenomenon of globalization. Having
witnessed the effects of secularism, materialism, consumerism, and
atheism on Latin America, Pope Francis knows that the decline of
Christian fervor and identity is not limited to the West.

The crisis in contemporary Christian culture and in culture in general reflects a pervasive, tragic loss of the encounter with Christ — and
the failure of Christians to facilitate that encounter. In an interview
with *Vatican Insider* during the consistory in February 2012, Cardinal Bergoglio was asked to describe the New Evangelization in Latin
America. He spoke in terms that are relevant to the whole Church:

> We need to avoid the spiritual sickness of a Church that is
> wrapped up in its own world: when a Church becomes like this,
> it grows sick. It is true that going out onto the street implies the
> risk of accidents happening, as they would to any ordinary man
> or woman. But if the Church stays wrapped up in itself, it will
> age. And if I had to choose between a wounded Church that goes
> out onto the streets and a sick withdrawn Church, I would defi-
> nitely choose the first one.

His pontificate with regard to the New Evangelization will be
both global and prophetic.

Global Catholicism

Pope Francis can see there is a crisis of culture, to be sure, and a
global Church facing a host of challenges, but the Church is also rich
in faith and in stories of the Gospel taking root and flourishing, even
in seemingly barren or rocky soil. The Church over the last fifty years

has doubled in size, from 527 million in 1959, to close to 1.3 billion today. The growth of Catholicism has also kept pace with the world's population, so that Catholics have remained about 17 percent of the total global population over those decades.

But the story of the Church today is not purely one of numbers, but rather of the shift from the Northern Hemisphere to the Southern Hemisphere, and to Asia, with tremendous implications for the coming years.

A century ago, there were one million Catholics in Africa, and almost all of them were Europeans. Fifty years ago, there were 21 million Catholics in Africa. Today, there are approximately 165 million Catholics, or 17.4 percent of the total population.

Similar numbers are seen in Asia and Latin America. The Catholic population as a percentage of the overall population of Asia is still quite small, barely 3 percent, but recent decades have seen huge growth in numbers. In India alone, the Catholic community has increased from five million fifty years ago to 18.5 million today, despite violence at the hands of radical Hindu political parties and the wider cultural traditions favoring Hinduism.

In South America, meanwhile, the Church is coping with anti-Catholic regimes in Cuba and Venezuela, materialism, native religions, and the loss of Catholics to Pentecostal churches. Still, the Church has more than kept pace with the growth of Latin America's population. In 1959, there were 31.5 million Mexican Catholics, while today there are 95 million. In Brazil, five decades ago there were 60 million Catholics, and today there are 179 million, although in both countries the percentages of Catholics have declined slightly.

The expansion of the Church in Africa, Asia, and Latin America is one of the great stories of evangelization in the last century, the fruits both of the Second Vatican Council and Pope John Paul II's pontificate. These trends are expected to continue this century. This is good news on many fronts, but it forces Catholics everywhere to face the ramifications of that success.

Africa. There are many threats to the continuing development of the Catholic faith in Africa. One of the most pressing is the fact that

┼

CATHOLIC POPULATIONS 1960-2010

	1960	2010
Africa	22,855,000	185,620,000
Europe	241,030,000	284,924,000
North America	106,874,000	246,981,000
South America	128,488,000	339,017,000
Asia	35,419,000	129,661,000
Oceania	2,867,000	9,468,000
World Total	537,533,000	1,195,671,000

(Sources: *Annuarium Statisticum Ecclesiae, Annuario Pontificio*, CSMC World Mission Map, 1960.)

across the continent conditions continue to deteriorate for Christians. In Nigeria, for example, thirteen states have declared Islamic *sharia* law will now govern them.

Other issues for the Church include: ethnic and religious strife; corruption and oppression by governments that hold back genuine economic development; furthering the process of inculturation for the acceptance of the faith within African culture; building new seminaries and schools; assisting Africans in stopping the spread of HIV/AIDS; and working to forge better ties between the Church and African governments and the African Union.

Asia. In his 1999 apostolic exhortation following the gathering of the Synod of Bishops on the Church in Asia, Pope John Paul II gave a concise overview of the grand sweep of the region, providing context for the work of the Church:

Asia is the earth's largest continent and is home to nearly two-thirds of the world's population, with China and India accounting for almost half the total population of the globe. The most striking feature of the continent is the variety of its peoples who are "heirs to ancient cultures, religions and traditions." We cannot but be amazed at the sheer size of Asia's population and at the intricate mosaic of its many cultures, languages, beliefs, and traditions, which comprise such a substantial part of the history and patrimony of the human family.

Asia is also the cradle of the world's major religions — Judaism, Christianity, Islam, and Hinduism. It is the birthplace of many other spiritual traditions such as Buddhism, Taoism, Confucianism, Zoroastrianism, Jainism, Sikhism, and Shintoism. Millions also espouse traditional or tribal religions, with varying degrees of structured ritual and formal religious teaching. The Church has the deepest respect for these traditions and seeks to engage in sincere dialogue with their followers. The religious values they teach await their fulfillment in Jesus Christ.

Today, Asia is home to millions of devout and zealous Catholics who nevertheless confront major issues. Lingering perceptions of Western colonialism, for example, have often left a legacy of bitterness and placed the Church at a disadvantage. Religious nationalism and intolerance are factors, too, in countries such as India and Bhutan, where churches are burned and vandalized on a regular basis, and Catholics can find it difficult to achieve justice from biased and disinterested authorities.

Pope John Paul II understood clearly the role of inculturation as a key element of the future for the Church. He wrote in his exhortation on Asia:

> In the process of encountering the world's different cultures, the Church not only transmits her truths and values and renews cultures from within, but she also takes from the various cultures the positive elements already found in them. This is the obligatory path for evangelizers in presenting the Christian faith and making it part of a people's cultural heritage. . . .
>
> This engagement with cultures has always been part of the Church's pilgrimage through history. But it has a special urgency today in the multiethnic, multi-religious and multicultural situation of Asia, where Christianity is still too often seen as foreign.

The Church in China, remarkably, represents potentially the greatest story for the Church in Asia. The Communist government has long sought to exercise control over the Church in China through the government-approved Chinese Patriotic Catholic Association. Officials have demanded the right to ordain bishops for the Church, for example, without the permission or approval of the Holy See. These ordinations have created formidable strains in the already difficult diplomatic relations, and yet the Church is flourishing.

It is difficult to know how many Chinese Catholics there are, but estimates place the population between eight million and twelve million. These Catholics are split between those who belong to the Patriotic Catholic Association and those who belong to the authentic Catholic Church. In some cases, Chinese Catholics may not even be aware of the fact that they belong to a parish that is part of the illegitimate Patriotic Association, and foreigners are also often unaware that they are attending Mass being celebrated by an illicitly ordained priest.

The Communist regime's efforts to control the Church are motivated in part by the steady increase in religious sentiment in China despite the country's officially atheist culture. The potential is there, of course, for Christianity to grow enormously if the Chinese government eventually allows genuine religious freedom.

Latin America. Meanwhile, the election of Pope Francis has changed the dynamic in relation to the Church in Latin America. The issues facing the Church there are daunting, chief among them: the lingering problems created by liberation theology; the political tilt to leftist and anti-Catholic governments; the staggering violence and chaos caused by drug cartels; endemic poverty in some regions; the dangers of secular materialism; mass migrations of people seeking work; and the loss of Catholics to Pentecostal churches, evangelical churches, and native religions.

The situation in Argentina illustrates some of these problems, as we have seen, but Venezuela and Brazil also provide examples. In Venezuela, the late leftist President Hugo Chavez came to power in 1998 and imposed state control of industry, curtailed civil and religious rights, and was not overly friendly to the Church and Church leaders. With his death Venezuela can choose to continue down its current path or it can reverse course.

Brazil — numerically the world's largest Catholic country — also labors under a leftist government, and there the Church also deals with aggressive proselytizing by evangelicals and the lure of materialism, atheism, and traditional religions such as Umbanda, an Afro-Brazilian religion that blends pagan rituals with elements of Catholic practice.

Middle East. In the Middle East and the lands where Islam is the dominant faith, a different set of problems has grown more urgent with every passing year. Currently, some 40 million Christians reside in countries ruled by Islamic governments, and many face legal, social, and economic discrimination, and even the chronic threat of violence and martyrdom. Christians in many of these areas were once the majority population, and the Christians cities of Alexandria, Antioch, and especially Constantinople were the cradles of Eastern Christianity and the home of many Church Fathers.

To be fair, there are many countries in which Christians exist with various freedoms and do not face persecution or severe legal and social disabilities, although frequently there are bans on proselytizing and conversion as well as restrictions on building places of worship. Several countries, such as Indonesia, Bangladesh, and Malaysia, have large non-Muslim populations, including Hindus, Christians, and Buddhists, who generally are allowed to practice their faith, build places of worship, and even enjoy some right to establish missionary centers.

However, several Islamic states — Algeria and Pakistan are examples — have imposed severe restrictions on Christians. Saudi Arabia bans all religions but Islam.

The phenomenon of Christians being forced to abandon their homes, cities, and even their countries is a growing one across the globe. It has assumed crisis proportions in the Middle East where in the last decade over three million Christians have left the Holy Land to settle in Europe, the United States, and Canada. As noted, they represent between a quarter to a third of all Christians living in the Middle East, the largest exodus of Christians from the area since the crusades of the twelfth and thirteenth centuries.

There were nearly 1.5 million Christians in Iraq at the start of the war there in 2003. Since then, Christians have been targeted for bombings, assassinations, and kidnappings, and most have fled to Syria, Jordan, Egypt, and Lebanon. It is estimated that only 500,000 Christians remain in Iraq. The exodus is not surprising given the fact that fundamentalism and general lawlessness in the country have led to the deaths of more than seven hundred Christians, and attacks on over seventy of their churches.

In Egypt, the Coptic Christians, who comprise 10 percent of the total population, have watched the so-called Arab Spring of 2011 sink into the Arab Winter. The Muslim Brotherhood — the radical Islamist party voted into power — has pushed ahead with a constitution that many critics see as an inevitable path to *sharia* law and the oppression of the Christian population.

In the face of the onslaught, Christian leaders in the region are concerned about preserving the Christian identity of their people. At the same time, these Christians belong to the wider body of 200 million Christians in more than 60 countries — such as China, Bhutan, and Cuba — who risk sometimes brutal retribution because of their faith.

————

The cardinals considered all of these issues as they prepared to enter the conclave to choose a successor to Benedict XVI. They shared their concerns in the general congregations and in their private conversations as they had also done at the different consistories over the last few years. And so the issues are familiar ones, and the 2007 Aparecida document mentioned earlier gives a sense of how Pope Francis will approach them:

> The Church is called to a deep and profound rethinking of its mission and to relaunch it with fidelity and boldness in the new circumstances of Latin America and the world. It cannot retreat in response to those who see only confusion, dangers, and threats, or those who seek to cloak the variety and complexity of situations with a mantle of worn-out ideological slogans or irresponsible attacks.
>
> What is required is confirming, renewing, and revitalizing the newness of the Gospel rooted in our history, out of a personal

and community encounter with Jesus Christ that raises up disciples and missionaries. That depends not so much on grand programs and structures, but rather on new men and women who incarnate that tradition and newness, as disciples of Jesus Christ and missionaries of his kingdom, protagonists of new life for a Latin America that seeks to be rediscovered with the light and power of the Spirit.

This will likely entail a threefold effort in Francis's pontificate:

- Finding allies among and encouraging outreach to the other faiths of the world and to women and men of goodwill.
- Recommitting the Church to evangelization that is centered completely on proclaiming Jesus Christ.
- Speaking and writing prophetically in the face of globalization and the persecution of Christians, reiterating the inviolable dignity of the human person and basic human rights.

Allies. As Pope Francis's pontificate unfolds, forging alliances with those institutions and faiths that hold similar views or at least share common ground will be of special interest.

Pope Benedict XVI enjoyed significant momentum in the area of ecumenical dialogue with the Orthodox churches, and the fruits of that dialogue were plain with the election of Francis. Russian Orthodox Patriarchate Kirill made very positive statements in the wake of the election of Francis, a sentiment shared with even greater enthusiasm by other Orthodox leaders, such as Ecumenical Patriarch Bartholomew of Constantinople and Metropolitan Tikhon, head of the Orthodox Church of America.

The general enthusiasm for the new pope was underscored by an unprecedented event: Patriarch Bartholomew became the first head of

---

✠

What is required is confirming, renewing, and revitalizing the newness of the Gospel rooted in our history, out of a personal and community encounter with Jesus Christ.

— APARECIDA DOCUMENT BY LATIN AMERICAN BISHOPS, 2007

the Greek Orthodox Church in nearly 1,000 years to attend the installation of a pope. Representatives of some twenty Christian churches and ecumenical organizations also attended the Installation Mass on March 19, but not since the 1054 schism between Catholics and Orthodox had the ecumenical patriarch come to Rome for the events marking the start of a new pontificate.

The Russian Orthodox Patriarchate, the largest of the Orthodox churches, sent Metropolitan Hilarion (Alfeyev) of Volokolamsk, the patriarchate's "foreign minister," to Francis's Installation Mass, but Hilarion made it clear in interviews that major issues remain between the two churches. A particularly critical issue is the presence of the Byzantine Catholic Church in Russia and Ukraine, which has been growing in numbers and was severely persecuted under the Soviet Union. Metropolitan Hilarion suggested that the pope should not give his support to Eastern-rite Catholics in Russia, an impossible proposition. (Interestingly, Cardinal Bergoglio had firsthand experience of the pastoral care of Eastern-rite Catholics, serving as their ordinary [bishop] in Argentina because they were without an ordinary of their own.)

Still, Francis's election prompted the Russian Orthodox to issue a statement that stressed: "The new pope is known for his conservative views, and his papacy will evidently be marked by the strengthening of faith. The fact that he has taken the name of Francis — reminiscent of Francis of Assisi — confirms his understanding of evangelization primarily as assistance for the poor and the deprived, as protection of their dignity."

Valery Shnyakin, deputy chairman of Russia's Federation Council Foreign Affairs Committee, told the Interfax News Agency that he hoped the election would propel dialogue forward, because "both the Russian Orthodox Church and the Catholic Church face similar threats. Morality is on the decline in society."

Cardinal Bergoglio's skill in relating to those of other faiths was evident in the excellent relations he enjoyed with Jewish and Islamic leaders in Argentina. He developed friendships with the heads of the local communities, even in a country where both faiths are tiny minorities. He opened the metropolitan cathedral for interfaith ser-

✢

The fact that he has taken the name of Francis — reminiscent of Francis of Assisi — confirms his understanding of evangelization primarily as assistance for the poor and the deprived, as protection of their dignity.

— STATEMENT OF THE RUSSIAN ORTHODOX CHURCH ON POPE FRANCIS

vices on several occasions, including the memorable evening in 2012 when a joint prayer service with the Jewish community commemorated the 74th anniversary of *Kristallnacht*, the night in Germany in 1938 when synagogues were destroyed throughout Germany, Jewish shops were looted, and thousands of Jews were arrested and deported to concentration camps.

Last November, Bergoglio invited representatives of the Muslim, Jewish, evangelical and Orthodox communities to the cathedral to pray for peace in the Middle East, and last December he happily lit the first candle on the menorah at Temple NCI-Emanu El during a Hanukkah ceremony in Buenos Aires. In 2006, in the aftermath of the controversy over Pope Benedict XVI's remarks at Regensburg, Germany, about the prophet Mohammad, he invited Muslims to an interfaith session. He did not preside, however, so that the media could not use the event as a direct criticism of Pope Benedict.

Outreach and dialogue likely will be a feature of the new pontificate, as they have been of Bergoglio's ministry over the years — sometimes in unexpected ways. Cardinal Bergoglio and his friend, Argentine Rabbi Abraham Skorka, for example, began a series of friendly debates on various relevant topics. They had so much fun that they decided to record the discussions and then co-authored a book, *Sobre el Cielo y la Tierra* (*On Heaven and Earth*). In it, Cardinal Bergoglio spoke of some features of interreligious dialogue, attitudes that are sure to inform his approach as pope:

> Dialogue is born from an attitude of respect for the other person, from a conviction that the other person has something good to say. It assumes that there is room in the heart for the other person's viewpoint, opinion, and ideas. Dialogue entails a cordial

reception, not a presumed condemnation. To carry out dialogue it is necessary to know how to lower the defenses, open the doors of the house, and offer human warmth. . . .

A religious leader can be very strong, very firm without exercising aggression. Jesus taught that the one who leads must be one who serves. For me, this idea is valid for the religious person of whatever religion.

Evangelization. Pope Francis sees the absolute importance of grounding all evangelization in Christ, a point that might seem obvious but is critical to his vision. The centrality of Christ has been a feature of the new pope's preaching for many years as he worked to make Christ visible to a world all too often shrouded in darkness and despair. He continued the theme in his first few homilies, saying on March 15 to the cardinals who had just elected him that "all of us" — the ordained and the laity — must "strive to respond faithfully to the Church's perennial mission: to bring Jesus Christ to mankind and to lead mankind to an encounter with Jesus Christ, the Way, the Truth and the Life, truly present in the Church and also in every person."

Human Dignity. Pope Francis will be a voice for the voiceless in the face of globalization, transnational capitalism, unrestrained free markets, and financial and economic policies rooted in greed or pride and that bring what he has called the "demonic effects of the imperialism of money." Globalization is a threat to most of the world's population — poor and largely unheard — through the economic colonialism of developed countries, the damage to God's creation, and the ruthless exploitation of cheap human labor. He touched briefly on these realities in his homily at the Installation Mass on March 19 when he called on everyone to be a protector in the footsteps of Saint Joseph, protector of Jesus and patron of the Church:

> The vocation of being a "protector," however, is not just something involving us Christians alone; it also has a prior dimension which is simply human, involving everyone. It means protecting all creation, the beauty of the created world, as the Book of Genesis tells us and as Saint Francis of Assisi showed us. It means

respecting each of God's creatures and respecting the environment in which we live.

It means protecting people, showing loving concern for each and every person, especially children, the elderly, those in need, who are often the last we think about.

Far from being a left-leaning theologian and supporter of liberation theology, Pope Francis rejects the politicization of the Church which distorts its ability to proclaim Jesus Christ. He stands squarely in the traditions of the Church's social doctrine that has developed with particular vigor over the last century, beginning with Pope Leo XIII's encyclical *Rerum Novarum*, the so-called Magna Carta of Catholic social teaching. During the Latin American bishops' meetings at Aparecida, Brazil, Bergoglio memorably said: "We live in the most unequal part of the world, which has grown the most, yet reduced misery the least. The unjust distribution of goods persists, creating a situation of social sin that cries out to heaven and limits the possibilities of a fuller life for so many of our brothers."

Finally, there is an unknown factor as the new pontificate gets underway: the impact of a pope from South America on Catholicism in the developing world. The first non-European since 731 and the first pontiff from the Southern Hemisphere, his election captivated Latin America. The churches there were filled with families praying for *Francisco*, including his old cathedral in Buenos Aires.

Jubilant crowds gathered outside the cathedral on the Plazo de Mayo, but vandals also gathered and defaced the building with graffiti, scrawling obscene messages about the pope and the Church. It was a symbol of the tension and the struggle between the forces of intolerant secularization and the Catholic faith, still relevant and central to the lives of countless Latin Americans.

But what about the world beyond South America and the Caribbean?

The pope's election brought joy across the whole of the Church. In Asia, Africa, the Middle East, and Oceania, his elevation to the papacy made it clear that the Church outside of Europe has matured and is now a cradle for a Successor to Saint Peter. Pope Francis, in his historic role, will have the opportunity to be a bridge builder, uniting the developed and the developing world, the continents of South America and Africa and Asia, and the Old World and the New World.

As Pope Benedict XVI observed at his own Installation Mass in 2005, the Church is alive and is young. Pope Francis comes from a region in which the Church is most definitely both. And he will be making apostolic journeys to parts of the world where vibrancy and youth will be on powerful display.

The world's median age is twenty-eight, but median ages are strikingly different depending upon the region. In the developed world the median age is thirty-nine, while in the developing world the average ages are anywhere from twenty-five down to nineteen, depending on the region. The median age of Africans is nineteen, Latin Americans twenty-six, and Asians twenty-seven. The Church is growing fastest in places where the world is youngest.

On the night of his election, the new pope asked for the prayers of the faithful. Saint Peter's Square fell silent as 150,000 women, men, and children, joined by hundreds of millions around the globe, prayed for their new Holy Father. To achieve his goals, Pope Francis will need the ongoing prayers of Catholics everywhere. He will also need their dedication to the task of evangelization, even in the face of persecution, calumny, mockery, and potential legal penalties for proclaiming Christ and the teaching of the Church.

As we have seen, Pope Francis has used the term "apostolic courage" to describe what the Church needs today: "To me apostolic courage is disseminating. Disseminating the Word. Giving it to that man and to that woman for whom it was bestowed. Giving them the beauty of the Gospel, the amazement of the encounter with Jesus . . . and leaving it to the Holy Spirit to do the rest. It is the Lord, says the Gospel, who makes the seed spring and bear fruit."

Reform and Renewal

As Pope Saint Gregory I the Great (d. 604) said, *"semper ecclesia reformanda"* ("the Church is always reforming"). Reform and renewal gathered steam in the pontificate of Benedict XVI, especially in matters involving the liturgy, the sex abuse crisis, and the central government of the Church. The absence of reform, or the failure to bring authentic reform and renewal, is more than a scandal; it creates terrible obstacles to the proclamation of Christ and the invitation to the world to encounter him in the Church. As the Synod of Bishops on the New Evangelization declared:

> The Church is the space offered by Christ in history where we can encounter him. . . . It is up to us today to render experiences of the Church concretely accessible, to multiply the wells where thirsting men and women are invited to encounter Jesus, to offer oases in the deserts of life. Christian communities and, in them, every disciple of the Lord are responsible for this: an irreplaceable testimony has been entrusted to each one, so that the Gospel can enter the lives of all. This requires of us holiness of life.

The welcoming community that must be the Church is wounded when its leaders are sources of scandal through careerism, vanity and pride, clericalism, and, worst of all, failures to deal with the perpetrators of sexual abuse according to the laws of the Church and the demands of authentic justice. The crisis of sexual abuse has led to great calamity for the victims and for the Church, and has been the source of immense heartache and frustration to faithful Catholics and to priests themselves, who have agonized over the monstrous crimes committed by the few.

Pope Francis assumes direction over a process of reform that began under Benedict XVI and that has achieved immense success in creating a safe environment for young people, in reforming seminary-formation programs, and in crafting universal norms for the handling of cases. Bergoglio has been a staunch advocate in Argentina for the protection of children in the face of sex trafficking, child abuse, and exploitation, and it can be anticipated that he will hold to this course.

In the book he co-authored with Rabbi Skorka, *Sobre el Cielo y la Tierra* (*On Heaven and Earth*), Cardinal Bergoglio spoke eloquently about his embrace of celibacy, but he also addressed the sex abuse crisis. He refuted the notion of celibacy as a root cause for abuse, but then he also announced his firm commitment to the zero-tolerance policy that had been established under Pope Benedict XVI. He said:

> You cannot be in a position of power and destroy the life of another person. In the diocese it never happened to me, but a bishop once called me to ask me by phone what to do in a situation like that, and I told him to take away the priests' licenses, not to allow them to exercise the priesthood any more, and to begin a canonical trial in that diocese's court. I think that's the attitude to have.
>
> I do not believe in taking positions that uphold a certain corporative spirit in order to avoid damaging the image of the institution. That solution was proposed once in the United States: they proposed switching the priests to a different parish. It is a stupid idea; that way, the priest just takes the problem with him wherever he goes. The corporate reaction leads to such a result, so I do not agree with those solutions. Recently, there were cases uncovered in Ireland from about twenty years ago, and the present pope [Benedict XVI] clearly said: "Zero tolerance for that crime." I admire the courage and uprightness of Pope Benedict on the subject.

In the days before the conclave, Cardinal Bergoglio spoke of the need for amendment and modernization in the Curia and in the administration of the Vatican, and it was well known that he tried to spend as little time as possible in Rome. According to the Vaticanista Sandro Magister, Bergoglio was once told that he might receive a major post as head of one of the congregations in the Curia. He reportedly replied, "Please no! Serving in the Curia would kill me." And yet he is also aware that the Curia is an important office at the service of the Petrine ministry and hence the Church. Cardinal Bergoglio spoke of this directly in an interview with *Vatican Insider* in 2012 when he described it as "a body that gives service, a body that helps me and serves me. Sometimes negative news does come out, but it is often exaggerated and manipulated to spread scandal. . . . The Roman Curia has its down sides, but I think that too much emphasis is placed on its negative aspects and not enough on the holiness of the numerous consecrated and laypeople who work in it."

In the same interview, he raised the connected issues of careerism and vanity. He warned that both reduce spiritual things to something worldly and added that those who are deep in self-absorbed vanity hide misery within.

Clericalism — an unhealthy attitude of separation and condescension by some priests toward those whom they are to serve — is connected to careerism and vanity. It was a specific source of concern for Cardinal Bergoglio who didn't hesitate to say of some priests in an interview with *30 Days*, "Their clericalization is a problem." In the same interview, he quoted the great twentieth-century theologian Henri de Lubac:

> It is what de Lubac calls "spiritual worldliness." It is the greatest danger for the Church, for us, who are in the Church. "It is worse," says de Lubac, "more disastrous than the infamous leprosy that disfigured the dearly beloved Bride at the time of the libertine popes." Spiritual worldliness is putting oneself at the center. It is what Jesus saw going on among the Pharisees: ". . .You who glorify yourselves. Who give glory to yourselves, the ones to the others."

Pope Francis's simplification of some protocols and his humble approach to his pontificate from the very first moments sent a clear message of his expectations for the entire Roman Curia, but also the entire Church. He made his commitment to reform apparent after his election. By custom, the new pope immediately confirms the heads of the dicasteries of the Roman Curia, all of whom had ceased to hold their positions at the start of the *sede vacante* because all officials serve entirely at the wish of the Holy Father. Pope Francis took an unusually long time to make the confirmation. Then the Vatican Press Office relayed the message that the Holy Father had confirmed that Vatican officials will continue in their various positions "*donec aliter provideatur*" ("until otherwise provided"), a formal and charged Vatican way of saying that changes might be coming.

If that was not plain enough, the second sentence of the communiqué read, "The Holy Father, in fact, wants to take a certain time for reflection, prayer, and dialogue before making any definitive appointments or confirmations." For Vatican observers, and perhaps for the party of reform in the College of Cardinals, it was a welcome, but also portentous, development that signaled progress toward the renewal they expect to see in the coming years.

———————

In April 2001, Cardinal Bergoglio, only recently made a cardinal, gave a talk at the Buenos Aires International Book Fair to mark the publication of the Spanish edition of *L'attrattiva Gesù* [*The Attraction of Jesus*], by Fr. Luigi Giussani. Giussani was the founder of the Communion and Liberation movement of which Bergoglio has long been a supporter. He focused on a theme that has resonated throughout his years of ministry and that serves as a final point of emphasis for where this unanticipated and unprecedented pontificate will take the Church in the coming years: the transforming encounter with Christ. The future pope said:

> Everything in our life, today just as in Jesus's time, begins with an encounter. An encounter with this Man, the carpenter of Nazareth, a man like all men and yet different. The first ones, John, Andrew, and Simon, felt themselves to be looked at into their very depths, read in their innermost being, and in them sprang forth a surprise, a wonder that instantly made them feel bound to him, made them feel different.
>
> When Jesus asked Peter, "Do you love Me?", "his 'Yes' was not the result of an effort of will, it was not the fruit of a 'decision' made by the young man Simon: it was the emergence, the coming to the surface of an entire vein of tenderness and adherence that made sense because of the esteem he had for him — therefore an act of reason"; it was a reasonable act, "which is why he couldn't not say 'Yes.'". . .
>
> Jesus is encountered, just as 2,000 years ago, in a human presence, the Church, the company of those whom he assimilates to himself, his body, the sign and sacrament of his Presence.
>
> He who encounters Jesus Christ feels the impulse to witness him or to give witness of what he has encountered, and this is the Christian calling. To go and give witness. You can't convince anybody. The encounter occurs. You can prove that God exists, but you will never be able, using the force of persuasion, to make

anyone encounter God. This is pure grace. Pure grace. In history, from its very beginning until today . . . grace always comes first, then comes all the rest.

EPILOGUE

---†---

It is not easy to entrust oneself to God's mercy, because it is an inscrutable abyss. But we must do it! "Oh, father, if you knew my life, you would not speak this way!" "Why, what have you done?" "Oh, I have done terrible things!" "All the better! Go to Jesus: he would be happy if you told him these things!" He forgets, he has a special capacity to forget. He forgets, he kisses you, he embraces you and he says to you: "Neither do I condemn you; go and from now on sin no more" (Jn 8:11). That is the only counsel he gives you. After a month, we are in the same situation. . . . Let us return to the Lord. The Lord never wearies of forgiving: never! We are the ones who grow weary of asking forgiveness. And let us ask for the grace to never weary of asking forgiveness because he never wearies of forgiving. Let us ask for this grace.

— Pope Francis, Homily at the Mass
at Saint Anne's in Vatican City, March 17, 2013

The face of God is that of a merciful father, who always has patience. Have you thought about God's patience, the patience that he has for each of us? That is his mercy. He always has patience, patience with us, he understands us, he waits for us, he does not weary of forgiving us if we know how to return to him with a contrite heart. Great is the mercy of the Lord, the Psalm says . . . mercy, this word changes everything. It is the best word we can hear: it changes the world. A little mercy makes the world less cold and more just. We need to rightly understand this mercy of God, this merciful Father, who has a lot of patience. . . . Let us remember the prophet Isaiah, who says that even if our sins are bright red, God's mercy can make them white as snow. Mercy is beautiful!

Let us not forget this: God never wearies of forgiving us, never! So, father, what's the problem? Well, the problem is that we grow weary, we do not want to, we tire of asking for forgiveness. He never tires of forgiving, but we, at times, we tire of asking forgiveness. Let us never tire, let us never tire! He is the loving Father, who always forgives, who has that heart of mercy for all of us. And we too learn to be merciful with everyone.

— POPE FRANCIS, ANGELUS, MARCH 17, 2013

ACKNOWLEDGMENTS

There are many individuals to whom I owe a special debt of gratitude for their kind assistance in the preparation of this book: Christine Owsik, OSV publicist; Jill Kurtz, John Christensen, Polly King, Kelly Lyons, and Cathy Dee of Our Sunday Visitor.

Thanks are owed also to York Young and Tyler Ottinger, both of Our Sunday Visitor, for their tireless work in the production phase, as well as to Sherri Hoffman, for her hard work in preparing the book for publication; and Greg Erlandson, president of Our Sunday Visitor, and Beth McNamara, editorial director of Our Sunday Visitor, for their unfailing support and inexplicable confidence that this project could be completed. Finally, I am especially grateful to Cindy Cavnar, my editor, for her boundless patience, imagination, and commitment to this project.

POPES OF THE
ROMAN CATHOLIC CHURCH

✠

Information includes the name of the pope, in many cases his name before becoming pope, his birthplace or country of origin, the date of accession to the papacy, and the date of the end of reign that, in all but a few cases, was the date of death. Double dates indicate date of election and date of solemn beginning of ministry as pastor of the universal Church. *Source*: *Annuario Pontificio*, Our Sunday Visitor's *Catholic Almanac*.

St. Peter (Simon Bar-Jona): Bethsaida in Galilee; d. c. 64 or 67.
St. Linus: Tuscany; 67-76.
St. Anacletus: Rome; 76-88.
St. Clement: Rome; 88-97.
St. Evaristus: Greece; 97-105.
St. Alexander I: Rome; 105-115.
St. Sixtus I: Rome; 115-125.
St. Telesphorus: Greece; 125-136.
St. Hyginus: Greece; 136-140.
St. Pius I: Aquileia; 140-155.
St. Anicetus: Syria; 155-166.
St. Soter: Campania; 166-175.
St. Eleutherius: Nicopolis in Epirus; 175-189.
St. Victor I: Africa; 189-199.
St. Zephyrinus: Rome; 199-217.
St. Callistus I: Rome; 217-222.
St. Urban I: Rome; 222-230.
St. Pontian: Rome; July 21, 230, to Sept. 28, 235.
St. Anterus: Greece; Nov. 21, 235, to Jan. 3, 236.
St. Fabian: Rome; Jan. 10, 236, to Jan. 20, 250.
St. Cornelius: Rome; Mar. 251 to June 253.
St. Lucius I: Rome; June 25, 253, to Mar. 5, 254.

St. Stephen I: Rome; May 12, 254, to Aug. 2, 257.

St. Sixtus II: Greece; Aug. 30, 257, to Aug. 6, 258.

St. Dionysius: birthplace unknown; July 22, 259, to Dec. 26, 268.

St. Felix I: Rome; Jan. 5, 269, to Dec. 30, 274.

St. Eutychian: Luni; Jan. 4, 275, to Dec. 7, 283.

St. Caius: Dalmatia; Dec. 17, 283, to Apr. 22, 296.

St. Marcellinus: Rome; June 30, 296, to Oct. 25, 304.

St. Marcellus I: Rome; May 27, 308, or June 26, 308, to Jan. 16, 309.

St. Eusebius: Greece; Apr. 18, 309, to Aug. 17, 309 or 310.

St. Melchiades (Miltiades): Africa; July 2, 311, to Jan. 11, 314.

St. Sylvester I: Rome; Jan. 31, 314, to Dec. 31, 335.

St. Marcus: Rome; Jan. 18, 336, to Oct. 7, 336.

St. Julius I: Rome; Feb. 6, 337, to Apr. 12, 352.

Liberius: Rome; May 17, 352, to Sept. 24, 366.

St. Damasus I: Spain; Oct. 1, 366, to Dec. 11, 384.

St. Siricius: Rome; Dec. 15, or 22 or 29, 384, to Nov. 26, 399.

St. Anastasius I: Rome; Nov. 27, 399, to Dec. 19, 401.

St. Innocent I: Albano; Dec. 22, 401, to Mar. 12, 417.

St. Zosimus: Greece; Mar. 18, 417, to Dec. 26, 418.

St. Boniface I: Rome; Dec. 28 or 29, 418, to Sept. 4, 422.

St. Celestine I: Campania; Sept. 10, 422, to July 27, 432.

St. Sixtus III: Rome; July 31, 432, to Aug. 19, 440.

St. Leo I the Great: Tuscany; Sept. 29, 440, to Nov. 10, 461.

St. Hilary: Sardinia; Nov. 19, 461, to Feb. 29, 468.

St. Simplicius: Tivoli; Mar. 3, 468, to Mar. 10, 483.

St. Felix III (II): Rome; Mar. 13, 483, to Mar. 1, 492.

St. Gelasius I: Africa; Mar. 1, 492, to Nov. 21, 496.

Anastasius II: Rome; Nov. 24, 496, to Nov. 19, 498.

St. Symmachus: Sardinia; Nov. 22, 498, to July 19, 514.

St. Hormisdas: Frosinone; July 20, 514, to Aug. 6, 523.

St. John I: Tuscany; Aug. 13, 523, to May 18, 526.

St. Felix IV (III): Samnium; July 12, 526, to Sept. 22, 530.

Boniface II: Rome; Sept. 22, 530, to Oct. 17, 532.

John II: Rome; Jan. 2, 533, to May 8, 535.

St. Agapitus I: Rome; May 13, 535, to Apr. 22, 536.

St. Silverius: Campania; June 1 or 8, 536, to Nov. 11, 537
    (d. Dec. 2, 537).

Vigilius: Rome; Mar. 29, 537, to June 7, 555.

Pelagius I: Rome; Apr. 16, 556, to Mar. 4, 561.

John III: Rome; July 17, 561, to July 13, 574.

Benedict I: Rome; June 2, 575, to July 30, 579.

Pelagius II: Rome; Nov. 26, 579, to Feb. 7, 590.

St. Gregory I the Great: Rome; Sept. 3, 590, to Mar. 12, 604.

Sabinian: Blera in Tuscany; Sept. 13, 604, to Feb. 22, 606.

Boniface III: Rome; Feb. 19, 607, to Nov. 12, 607.

St. Boniface IV: Abruzzi; Aug. 25, 608, to May 8, 615.

St. Deusdedit (Adeodatus I): Rome; Oct. 19, 615, to Nov. 8, 618.

Boniface V: Naples; Dec. 23, 619, to Oct. 25, 625.

Honorius I: Campania; Oct. 27, 625, to Oct. 12, 638.

Severinus: Rome; May 28, 640, to Aug. 2, 640.

John IV: Dalmatia; Dec. 24, 640, to Oct. 12, 642.

Theodore I: Greece; Nov. 24, 642, to May 14, 649.

St. Martin I: Todi; July, 649, to Sept. 16, 655
    (in exile from June 17, 653).

St. Eugene I: Rome; Aug. 10, 654, to June 2, 657.

St. Vitalian: Segni; July 30, 657, to Jan. 27, 672.

Adeodatus II: Rome; Apr. 11, 672, to June 17, 676.

Donus: Rome; Nov. 2, 676, to Apr. 11, 678.

St. Agatho: Sicily; June 27, 678, to Jan. 10, 681.

St. Leo II: Sicily; Aug. 17, 682, to July 3, 683.

St. Benedict II: Rome; June 26, 684, to May 8, 685.

John V: Syria; July 23, 685, to Aug. 2, 686.

Conon: birthplace unknown; Oct. 21, 686, to Sept. 21, 687.

St. Sergius I: Syria; Dec. 15, 687, to Sept. 8, 701.

John VI: Greece; Oct. 30, 701, to Jan. 11, 705.

John VII: Greece; Mar. 1, 705, to Oct. 18, 707.

Sisinnius: Syria; Jan. 15, 708, to Feb. 4, 708.

Constantine: Syria; Mar. 25, 708, to Apr. 9, 715.

St. Gregory II: Rome; May 19, 715, to Feb. 11, 731.

St. Gregory III: Syria; Mar. 18, 731, to Nov. 741.

St. Zachary: Greece; Dec. 10, 741, to Mar. 22, 752.

Stephen II (III): Rome; Mar. 26, 752, to Apr. 26, 757.

St. Paul I: Rome; Apr. (May 29), 757, to June 28, 767.

Stephen III (IV): Sicily; Aug. 1 (7), 768, to Jan. 24, 772.

Adrian I: Rome; Feb. 1 (9), 772, to Dec. 25, 795.

St. Leo III: Rome; Dec. 26 (27), 795, to June 12, 816.

Stephen IV (V): Rome; June 22, 816, to Jan. 24, 817.

St. Paschal I: Rome; Jan. 25, 817, to Feb. 11, 824.

Eugene II: Rome; Feb. (May) 824 to Aug. 827.

Valentine: Rome; Aug. 827, to Sept. 827.

Gregory IV: Rome; 827, to Jan. 844.

Sergius II: Rome; Jan. 844 to Jan. 27, 847.

St. Leo IV: Rome; Jan. (Apr. 10) 847, to July 17, 855.

Benedict III: Rome; July (Sept. 29), 855, to Apr. 17, 858.

St. Nicholas I the Great: Rome; Apr. 24, 858, to Nov. 13, 867.

Adrian II: Rome; Dec. 14, 867, to Dec. 14, 872.

John VIII: Rome; Dec. 14, 872, to Dec. 16, 882.

Marinus I: Gallese; Dec. 16, 882, to May 15, 884.

St. Adrian III: Rome; May 17, 884, to Sept. 885.

Stephen V (VI): Rome; Sept. 885, to Sept. 14, 891.

Formosus: Bishop of Porto; Oct. 6, 891, to Apr. 4, 896.

Boniface VI: Rome; Apr. 896 to Apr. 896.

Stephen VI (VII): Rome; May 896 to Aug. 897.

Romanus: Gallese; Aug. 897 to Nov. 897.

Theodore II: Rome; Dec. 897 to Dec. 897.

John IX: Tivoli; Jan. 898 to Jan. 900.

Benedict IV: Rome; Jan. (Feb.) 900 to July 903.

Leo V: Ardea; July 903 to Sept. 903.

Sergius III: Rome; Jan. 29, 904, to Apr. 14, 911.

Anastasius III: Rome; Apr. 911 to June 913.

Landus: Sabina; July 913 to Feb. 914.

John X: Tossignano (Imola); Mar. 914 to May 928.

Leo VI: Rome; May 928 to Dec. 928.

Stephen VII (VIII): Rome; Dec. 928 to Feb. 931.

John XI: Rome; Feb. (Mar.) 931 to Dec. 935.

Leo VII: Rome; Jan. 3, 936, to July 13, 939.

Stephen VIII (IX): Rome; July 14, 939, to Oct. 942.

Marinus II: Rome; Oct. 30, 942, to May 946.

Agapitus II: Rome; May 10, 946, to Dec. 955.

John XII (Octavius): Tusculum; Dec. 16, 955, to May 14, 964 (date of his death).

Leo VIII: Rome; Dec. 4 (6), 963, to Mar. 1, 965.

Benedict V: Rome; May 22, 964, to July 4, 966.

John XIII: Rome; Oct. 1, 965, to Sept. 6, 972.

Benedict VI: Rome; Jan. 19, 973 to June 974.

Benedict VII: Rome; Oct. 974 to July 10, 983.

John XIV (Peter Campenora): Pavia; Dec., 983 to Aug. 20, 984.

John XV: Rome; Aug. 985 to Mar. 996.

Gregory V (Bruno of Carinthia): Saxony; May 3, 996, to Feb. 18, 999.

Sylvester II (Gerbert): Auvergne; Apr. 2, 999, to May 12, 1003.

John XVII (Siccone): Rome; June 1003 to Dec. 1003.

John XVIII (Phasianus): Rome; Jan. 1004, to July 1009.

Sergius IV (Peter): Rome; July 31, 1009, to May 12, 1012.

Benedict VIII (Theophylactus): Tusculum; May 18, 1012,
    to Apr. 9, 1024.

John XIX (Romanus): Tusculum; Apr. (May) 1024 to 1032.

Benedict IX (Theophylactus): Tusculum; 1032 to 1044.

Sylvester III (John): Rome; Jan. 20, 1045, to Feb. 10, 1045.

Benedict IX (second time): Apr. 10, 1045, to May 1, 1045.

Gregory VI (John Gratian): Rome; May 5, 1045, to Dec. 20, 1046.

Clement II (Suitger, Lord of Morsleben and Hornburg): Saxony;
    Dec. 24 (25), 1046 to Oct. 9, 1047.

Benedict IX (third time): Nov. 8, 1047, to July 17, 1048 (d. c. 1055).

Damasus II (Poppo): Bavaria; July 17, 1048, to Aug. 9, 1048.

St. Leo IX (Bruno): Alsace; Feb. 12, 1049, to Apr. 19, 1054.

Victor II (Gebhard): Swabia; Apr. 16, 1055, to July 28, 1057.

Stephen IX (X) (Frederick): Lorraine; Aug. 3, 1057, to Mar. 29, 1058.

Nicholas II (Gerard): Burgundy; Jan. 24, 1059, to July 27, 1061.

Alexander II (Anselmo da Baggio): Milan; Oct. 1, 1061,
    to Apr. 21, 1073.

St. Gregory VII (Hildebrand): Tuscany; Apr. 22 (June 30), 1073,
    to May 25, 1085.

Bl. Victor III (Dauferius; Desiderius): Benevento; May 24, 1086,
    to Sept. 16, 1087.

Bl. Urban II (Otto di Lagery): France; Mar. 12, 1088, to July 29, 1099.

Paschal II (Raniero): Ravenna; Aug. 13 (14), 1099, to Jan. 21, 1118.

Gelasius II (Giovanni Caetani): Gaeta; Jan. 24 (Mar. 10), 1118,
    to Jan. 28, 1119.

Callistus II (Guido of Burgundy): Burgundy; Feb. 2 (9), 1119,
to Dec. 13, 1124.

Honorius II (Lamberto): Fiagnano (Imola); Dec. 15 (21), 1124,
to Feb. 13, 1130.

Innocent II (Gregorio Papareschi): Rome; Feb. 14 (23), 1130,
to Sept. 24, 1143.

Celestine II (Guido): Citta di Castello; Sept. 26 (Oct. 3), 1143,
to Mar. 8, 1144.

Lucius II (Gerardo Caccianemici): Bologna: Mar. 12, 1144,
to Feb. 15, 1145.

Bl. Eugene III (Bernardo Paganelli di Montemagno): Pisa; Feb. 15 (18),
1145, to July 8, 1153.

Anastasius IV (Corrado): Rome; July 12, 1153, to Dec, 3, 1154.

Adrian IV (Nicholas Breakspear): England; Dec. 4 (5), 1154,
to Sept. 1, 1159.

Alexander III (Rolando Bandinelli): Siena; Sept. 7 (20), 1159,
to Aug. 30, 1181.

Lucius III (Ubaldo Allucingoli): Lucca; Sept. 1 (6), 1181,
to Sept. 25, 1185.

Urban III (Uberto Crivelli): Milan; Nov. 25 (Dec. 1), 1185,
to Oct. 20, 1187.

Gregory VIII (Alberto de Morra): Benevento; Oct. 21 (25), 1187,
to Dec. 17, 1187.

Clement III (Paolo Scolari): Rome; Dec. 19 (20), 1187, to Mar. 1191.

Celestine III (Giacinto Bobone): Rome; Mar. 30 (Apr. 14), 1191,
to Jan. 8, 1198.

Innocent III (Lotario dei Conti di Segni); Anagni; Jan. 8 (Feb. 22),
1198, to July 16, 1216.

Honorius III (Cencio Savelli): Rome; July 18 (24), 1216,
to Mar. 18, 1227.

Gregory IX (Ugolino, Count of Segni): Anagni; Mar. 19 (21), 1227,
to Aug. 22, 1241.

Celestine IV (Goffredo Castiglioni): Milan; Oct. 25 (28), 1241,
to Nov. 10, 1241.

Innocent IV (Sinibaldo Fieschi): Genoa; June 25 (28), 1243,
to Dec. 7, 1254.

Alexander IV (Rinaldo, House of Ienne): Ienne (Rome); Dec. 12 (20), 1254, to May 25, 1261.

Urban IV (Jacques Pantaléon): Troyes; Aug. 29 (Sept. 4), 1261, to Oct. 2, 1264.

Clement IV (Guy Foulques or Guido le Gros): France; Feb. 5 (15), 1265, to Nov. 29, 1268.

Bl. Gregory X (Teobaldo Visconti): Piacenza; Sept. 1, 1271 (Mar. 27, 1272), to Jan. 10, 1276.

Bl. Innocent V (Peter of Tarentaise): Savoy; Jan. 21 (Feb. 22), 1276, to June 22, 1276.

Adrian V (Ottobono Fieschi): Genoa: July 11, 1276, to Aug. 18, 1276.

John XXI (Petrus Juliani or Petrus Hispanus): Portugal; Sept. 8 (20), 1276, to May 20, 1277.

Nicholas III (Giovanni Gaetano Orsini): Rome; Nov. 25 (Dec. 26), 1277, to Aug. 22, 1280.

Martin IV (Simon de Brie): France; Feb. 22 (Mar. 23), 1281, to Mar. 28, 1285.

Honorius IV (Giacomo Savelli): Rome; Apr. 2 (May 20), 1285, to Apr. 3, 1287.

Nicholas IV (Girolamo Masci): Ascoli; Feb. 22, 1288, to Apr. 4, 1292.

St. Celestine V (Pietro del Murrone): Isernia; July 5 (Aug. 29), 1294, to Dec. 13, 1294; d. May 19, 1296.

Boniface VIII (Benedetto Caetani): Anagni; Dec. 24, 1294 (Jan. 23, 1295), to Oct. 11, 1303.

Bl. Benedict XI (Niccolo Boccasini): Treviso; Oct. 22 (27), 1303, to July 7, 1304.

Clement V (Bertrand de Got): France; June 5 (Nov. 14), 1305, to Apr. 20, 1314.

John XXII (Jacques d'Euse): Cahors; Aug. 7 (Sept. 5), 1316, to Dec. 4, 1334.

Benedict XII (Jacques Fournier): France; Dec. 20, 1334 (Jan. 8, 1335), to Apr. 25, 1342.

Clement VI (Pierre Roger): France; May 7 (19), 1342, to Dec. 6, 1352.

Innocent VI (Etienne Aubert): France; Dec. 18 (30), 1352, to Sept. 12, 1362.

Bl. Urban V (Guillaume de Grimoard): France; Sept. 28 (Nov. 6), 1362, to Dec. 19, 1370.

Gregory XI (Pierre Roger de Beaufort): France; Dec. 30, 1370 (Jan. 5, 1371), to Mar. 26, 1378.

Urban VI (Bartolomeo Prignano): Naples; Apr. 8 (18), 1378, to Oct. 15, 1389.

Boniface IX (Pietro Tomacelli): Naples; Nov. 2 (9), 1389, to Oct. 1, 1404.

Innocent VII (Cosma Migliorati): Sulmona; Oct. 17 (Nov. 11), 1404, to Nov. 6, 1406.

Gregory XII (Angelo Correr): Venice; Nov. 30 (Dec. 19), 1406, to July 4, 1415, when he voluntarily resigned from the papacy to permit the election of his successor. He died Oct. 18, 1417.

Martin V (Oddone Colonna): Rome; Nov. 11 (21), 1417, to Feb. 20, 1431.

Eugene IV (Gabriele Condulmer): Venice; Mar. 3 (11), 1431, to Feb. 23, 1447.

Nicholas V (Tommaso Parentucelli): Sarzana; Mar. 6 (19), 1447, to Mar. 24, 1455.

Callistus III (Alfonso Borgia): Jativa (Valencia); Apr. 8 (20), 1455, to Aug. 6, 1458.

Pius II (Enea Silvio Piccolomini): Siena; Aug. 19 (Sept. 3), 1458, to Aug. 14, 1464.

Paul II (Pietro Barbo): Venice; Aug. 30 (Sept. 16), 1464, to July 26, 1471.

Sixtus IV (Francesco della Rovere): Savona; Aug. 9 (25), 1471, to Aug. 12, 1484.

Innocent VIII (Giovanni Battista Cibo): Genoa; Aug. 29 (Sept. 12), 1484, to July 25, 1492.

Alexander VI (Rodrigo Borgia): Jativa (Valencia); Aug. 11 (26), 1492, to Aug. 18, 1503.

Pius III (Francesco Todeschini-Piccolomini): Siena; Sept. 22 (Oct. 1, 8), 1503, to Oct. 18, 1503.

Julius II (Giuliano della Rovere): Savona; Oct. 31 (Nov. 26), 1503, to Feb. 21, 1513.

Leo X (Giovanni de' Medici): Florence; Mar. 9 (19), 1513, to Dec. 1, 1521.

Adrian VI (Adrian Florensz): Utrecht; Jan. 9 (Aug. 31), 1522, to Sept. 14, 1523.

Clement VII (Giulio de' Medici): Florence; Nov. 19 (26), 1523,
to Sept. 25, 1534.

Paul III (Alessandro Farnese): Rome; Oct. 13 (Nov. 3), 1534,
to Nov. 10, 1549.

Julius III (Giovanni Maria Ciocchi del Monte): Rome; Feb. 7 (22),
1550, to Mar. 23, 1555.

Marcellus II (Marcello Cervini): Montepulciano; Apr. 9 (10), 1555,
to May 1, 1555.

Paul IV (Gian Pietro Carafa): Naples; May 23 (26), 1555,
to Aug. 18, 1559.

Pius IV (Giovan Angelo de' Medici): Milan; Dec. 25, 1559
(Jan. 6, 1560), to Dec. 9, 1565.

St. Pius V (Antonio-Michele Ghislieri): Bosco (Alexandria); Jan. 7 (17),
1566, to May 1, 1572.

Gregory XIII (Ugo Buoncompagni): Bologna; May 13 (25), 1572,
to Apr. 10, 1585.

Sixtus V (Felice Peretti): Grottammare (Ripatransone); Apr. 24
(May 1), 1585, to Aug. 27, 1590.

Urban VII (Giambattista Castagna): Rome; Sept. 15, 1590,
to Sept. 27, 1590.

Gregory XIV (Niccolo Sfondrati): Cremona; Dec. 5 (8), 1590,
to Oct. 16, 1591.

Innocent IX (Giovanni Antonio Facchinetti): Bologna; Oct. 29
(Nov. 3), 1591, to Dec. 30, 1591.

Clement VIII (Ippolito Aldobrandini): Florence; Jan. 30 (Feb. 9), 1592,
to Mar. 3, 1605.

Leo XI (Alessandro de' Medici): Florence; Apr. 1 (10), 1605,
to Apr. 27, 1605.

Paul V (Camillo Borghese): Rome; May 16 (29), 1605, to Jan. 28, 1621.

Gregory XV (Alessandro Ludovisi): Bologna; Feb. 9 (14), 1621,
to July 8, 1623.

Urban VIII (Maffeo Barberini): Florence; Aug. 6 (Sept. 29), 1623,
to July 29, 1644.

Innocent X (Giovanni Battista Pamfili): Rome; Sept. 15 (Oct. 4), 1644,
to Jan. 7, 1655.

Alexander VII (Fabio Chigi): Siena; Apr. 7 (18), 1655, to May 22, 1667.

Clement IX (Giulio Rospigliosi): Pistoia; June 20 (26), 1667,
    to Dec. 9, 1669.
Clement X (Emilio Altieri): Rome; Apr. 29 (May 11), 1670,
    to July 22, 1676.
Bl. Innocent XI (Benedetto Odescalchi): Como; Sept. 21 (Oct. 4),
    1676, to Aug. 12, 1689.
Alexander VIII (Pietro Ottoboni): Venice; Oct. 6 (16), 1689,
    to Feb. 1, 1691.
Innocent XII (Antonio Pignatelli): Spinazzola (Venosa); July 12 (15),
    1691, to Sept. 27, 1700.
Clement XI (Giovanni Francesco Albani): Urbino; Nov. 23, 30
    (Dec. 8), 1700, to Mar. 19, 1721.
Innocent XIII (Michelangelo dei Conti): Rome; May 8 (18), 1721,
    to Mar. 7, 1724.
Benedict XIII (Pietro Francesco Vincenzo Maria Orsini): Gravina
    (Bari); May 29 (June 4), 1724, to Feb. 21, 1730.
Clement XII (Lorenzo Corsini): Florence; July 12 (16), 1730,
    to Feb. 6, 1740.
Benedict XIV (Prospero Lambertini): Bologna; Aug. 17 (22), 1740,
    to May 3, 1758.
Clement XIII (Carlo Rezzonico): Venice; July 6 (16), 1758,
    to Feb. 2, 1769.
Clement XIV (Giovanni Vincenzo Antonio Lorenzo Ganganelli):
    Rimini; May 19, 28 (June 4), 1769, to Sept. 22, 1774.
Pius VI (Giovanni Angelo Braschi): Cesena; Feb. 15 (22), 1775,
    to Aug. 29, 1799.
Pius VII (Barnaba Gregorio Chiaramonti): Cesena; Mar. 14 (21), 1800,
    to Aug. 20, 1823.
Leo XII (Annibale della Genga): Genga (Fabriano); Sept. 28 (Oct. 5),
    1823, to Feb. 10, 1829.
Pius VIII (Francesco Saverio Castiglioni): Cingoli; Mar. 31 (Apr. 5),
    1829, to Nov. 30, 1830.
Gregory XVI (Bartolomeo Alberto-Mauro-Cappellari): Belluno;
    Feb. 2 (6), 1831, to June 1, 1846.
Bl. Pius IX (Giovanni M. Mastai-Ferretti): Senigallia; June 16 (21),
    1846, to Feb. 7, 1878.

Leo XIII (Gioacchino Pecci): Carpineto (Anagni); Feb. 20 (Mar. 3), 1878, to July 20, 1903.

St. Pius X (Giuseppe Sarto): Riese (Treviso); Aug. 4 (9), 1903, to Aug. 20, 1914. Canonized May 29, 1954.

Benedict XV (Giacomo della Chiesa): Genoa; Sept. 3 (6), 1914, to Jan. 22, 1922.

Pius XI (Achille Ratti): Desio (Milan); Feb. 6 (12), 1922, to Feb. 10, 1939.

Pius XII (Eugenio Pacelli): Rome; Mar. 2 (12), 1939, to Oct. 9, 1958.

Bl. John XXIII (Angelo Giuseppe Roncalli): Sotto il Monte (Bergamo); Oct. 28 (Nov. 4), 1958, to June 3, 1963.

Paul VI (Giovanni Battista Montini): Concessio (Brescia); June 21 (30), 1963, to Aug. 6, 1978.

John Paul I (Albino Luciani): Forno di Canale (Belluno); Aug. 26 (Sept. 3), 1978, to Sept. 28, 1978.

John Paul II (Karol Wojtyla): Wadowice, Poland; Oct. 16 (22), 1978, to April 2, 2005.

Benedict XVI (Joseph Ratzinger): Marktl am Inn, Germany; April 19 (24), 2005 to Feb. 28, 2013.

Francis (Jorge Mario Bergoglio: Buenos Aires, Argentina; March 13 (19), 2013 to present.

GLOSSARY

—✠—

Aggiornamento: An Italian word having the general meaning of bringing up to date, renewal, revitalization, descriptive of the processes of spiritual renewal and institutional reform and change in the Church; fostered by the Second Vatican Council.

Apostolic Succession: Bishops of the Church, who form a collective body or college, are successors to the apostles by ordination and divine right; as such they carry on the mission entrusted by Christ to the apostles as guardians and teachers of the deposit of faith, principal pastors and spiritual authorities of the faithful. The doctrine of apostolic succession is based on New Testament evidence and the constant teaching of the Church, reflected as early as the end of the first century in a letter of Pope Saint Clement to the Corinthians. A significant facet of the doctrine is the role of the pope as the successor of Saint Peter, the Vicar of Christ and head of the college of bishops. The doctrine of apostolic succession means more than continuity of apostolic faith and doctrine; its basic requisite is ordination by the laying on of hands in apostolic succession.

Authority, Ecclesiastical: The authority exercised by the Church, and particularly by the pope and the bishops; it is delegated by Jesus Christ to Saint Peter. This authority extends to all those matters entrusted to the apostles by Christ, including teaching of the Faith, the liturgy and sacraments, moral guidance, and the administration of discipline.

Baldacchino: A canopy over an altar.

Biglietto: A papal document of notification of appointment to the cardinalate.

Blessing: Invocation of God's favor, by official ministers of the Church or by private individuals. Blessings are recounted in the Old and New Testaments, and are common in the Christian tradition. Many types of blessings are listed in the Book of Blessings of the Roman Ritual. Private blessings, as well as those of an official kind, are efficacious. Blessings are imparted with the Sign of the Cross and appropriate prayer.

Brief, Apostolic: A papal letter, less formal than a bull, signed for the pope by a secretary and impressed with the seal of the Fisherman's Ring. Simple apostolic letters of this kind are issued for beatifications and with respect to other matters.

Bull, Apostolic: Apostolic letter, a solemn form of papal document, beginning with the name and title of the pope (e.g., John Paul II, Servant of the Servants of God), dealing with an important subject, sealed with a *bulla* or red-ink imprint of the device on the *bulla*. Bulls are issued to confer the titles of bishops and cardinals, to promulgate canonizations, to proclaim Holy Years and for other purposes. A collection of bulls is called a *bullarium*.

Camerlengo **(Chamberlain):** (1) the Chamberlain of the Holy Roman Church is a cardinal with special responsibilities, especially during the time between the death of one pope and the election of his successor; among other things, he safeguards and administers the goods and revenues of the Holy See and heads particular congregations of cardinals for special purposes. (2) the Chamberlain of the College of Cardinals has charge of the property and revenues of the College and keeps the record of business transacted in consistories. (3) the Chamberlain of the Roman Clergy is the president of the secular clergy of Rome.

Canon Law: The Code of Canon Law (*Corpus Iuris Canonici*) enacted and promulgated by ecclesiastical authority for the orderly and pastoral administration and government of the Church. A revised Code for the Latin rite, effective Novevmber 27, 1983, consists of 1,752 canons in seven books under the titles of general norms, the people of God, the teaching mission of the Church, the sanctifying mission of the Church, temporal goods of the Church, penal law, and procedural law. The antecedent of this Code was promulgated in 1917 and became effective in 1918; it consisted of 2,414 canons in five books covering general rules, ecclesiastical persons, sacred things, trials, crimes and punishments. There is a separate Code of the Canons of Eastern Churches, in effect since October 1, 1991.

Cardinal: Member of the sacred College of Cardinals and a high-ranking, powerful member of the Church hierarchy. He gives assistance to the pope in the government of the Church and has the important task of taking part in the election of a new successor of Saint

Peter. By canon law, all cardinals must be ordained priests; those who are not bishops at the time of their elevation are consecrated to the episcopacy.

Catechism: A systematic presentation of the fundamentals of Catholic doctrine regarding faith and morals. Sources are Sacred Scripture, tradition, the magisterium (teaching authority of the Church), the writings of Fathers and Doctors of the Church, liturgy. The new *Catechism of the Catholic Church*, published October 11, 1992, consists of four principal sections: the profession of faith (the Creed), the sacraments of faith, the life of faith (the Commandments), and the prayer of the believer (the Lord's Prayer). The sixteenth-century Council of Trent mandated publication of the *Roman Catechism*. Catechisms such as these two are useful sources for other catechisms serving particular needs of the faithful and persons seeking admission to the Catholic Church.

Cathedra: A Greek word for chair, designating the chair or seat of a bishop in the principal church of his diocese, which is therefore called a cathedral.

Catholic: A Greek word, meaning universal, first used in the title Catholic Church in a letter written by Saint Ignatius of Antioch about 107 to the Christians of Smyrna.

Ceremonies, Master of: One who directs the proceedings of a rite or ceremony during that function. The Papal Master of Ceremonies has responsibility for organizing all papal liturgies.

Chirograph or Autograph Letter: A letter written by a pope himself, in his own handwriting.

Christology: Branch of theology concerned with the person and nature of Jesus Christ, with particular attention paid to his Divine Person and his two natures, human and divine. It should not be confused with soteriology, the branch of theology concerned with Christ's labors of salvation.

Clergy: Men ordained to holy orders and commissioned for sacred ministries and assigned to pastoral and other duties for the service of the people and the Church: (1) Diocesan or secular clergy are committed to pastoral ministry in parishes and in other capacities in a particular church (diocese) under the direction of their bishop, to whom they are bound by a promise of obedience. (2) Regular clergy belong to religious institutes (orders, congregations, societies — institutes of consecrated life) and are so called because they observe the rule (*regula*, in Latin) of their respective institutes. They are committed to the ways of life and apostolates of their institutes. In ordinary pastoral ministry, they are under the direction of local bishops as well as their own superiors.

Collegiality: A term in use especially since the Second Vatican Council to describe the authority exercised by the College of Bishops. The bishops of the Church, in union with and subordinate to the pope — who has full, supreme and universal power over the Church which he can always exercise independently — have supreme teaching and pastoral authority over the whole Church. In addition to their proper authority of office for the good of the faithful in their respective dioceses or other jurisdictions, the bishops have authority to act for the good of the universal Church. This collegial authority is exercised in a solemn manner in an ecumenical council and can also be exercised in other ways sanctioned by the pope. Doctrine on collegiality was set forth by the Second Vatican Council in *Lumen Gentium* (the Dogmatic Constitution on the Church). (See separate entry.) By extension, the concept of collegiality is applied to other forms of participation and co-responsibility by members of a community.

Conclave: The term used for the formal gathering of the members of the College of Cardinals to elect a new pope. The name, taken from the Latin, *cum clavis* ("with a key"), is derived from the fact that since 1274 the cardinals are sequestered until they reach a decision on the new successor to Saint Peter. Only cardinals under the age of 80 are eligible to participate. Starting with the conclave of 1878, every such gathering has been held in the Sistine Chapel.

Concordat: A church-state treaty with the force of law concerning matters of mutual concern — for example, rights of the Church, arrangement of ecclesiastical jurisdictions, marriage laws, education. Approximately 150 agreements of this kind have been negotiated since the Concordat of Worms in 1122.

Congregation: (1) The collective name for the people who form a parish. (2) One of the chief administrative departments of the Roman Curia. (3) An unofficial term for a group of men and women who belong to a religious community or institute of consecrated life.

Consistory: An assembly of cardinals presided over by the pope.

Constitution: (1) An apostolic or papal constitution is a document in which a pope enacts and promulgates law. (2) A formal and solemn document issued by an ecumenical council on a doctrinal or pastoral subject, with binding force in the whole Church; e.g., the four constitutions issued by the Second Vatican Council on the Church, liturgy, revelation, and the Church in the modern world. (3) The constitutions of institutes of consecrated life and societies of apostolic life spell out details of and norms drawn from the various rules for the guidance and direction of the life and work of their members.

Council: A formal meeting of Church leaders, summoned by a bishop or appropriate Church leader, with the general purpose of assisting the life of the Church through deliberations, decrees, and promulgations. Different councils include: diocesan councils (synod), a gathering of the officials of an individual diocese; provincial councils, the meeting of the bishops of a province; plenary councils, the assembly of the bishops of a country; and ecumenical councils, a gathering of all the bishops in the world under the authority of the Bishop of Rome.

Crosier: The bishop's staff, symbolic of his pastoral office, responsibility and authority, used at liturgical functions.

Crypt: An underground or partly underground chamber; e.g., the lower part of a church used for worship and/or burial.

Cura Animarum: A Latin phrase, meaning care of souls, designating the pastoral ministry and responsibility of bishops and priests.

Curia: The personnel and offices through which (1) the pope administers the affairs of the universal Church, the Roman Curia, or (2) a bishop the affairs of a diocese, diocesan curia. The principal officials of a diocesan curia are the vicar general of the diocese, the chancellor, officials of the diocesan tribunal or court, examiners, consultors, auditors, notaries.

Dean: (1) A priest with supervisory responsibility over a section of a diocese known as a deanery. The post-Vatican II counterpart of a dean is an episcopal vicar. (2) The senior or ranking member of a group.

Declaration: (1) An ecclesiastical document which presents an interpretation of an existing law. (2) A position paper on a specific subject;

e.g., the three declarations issued by the Second Vatican Council on religious freedom, non-Christian religions, and Christian education.

Decree: An edict or ordinance issued by a pope and/or by an ecumenical council, with binding force in the whole Church; by a department of the Roman Curia, with binding force for concerned parties; by a territorial body of bishops, with binding force for persons in the area; by individual bishops, with binding force for concerned parties until revocation or the death of the bishop. The nine decrees issued by the Second Vatican Council were combinations of doctrinal and pastoral statements with executive orders for action and movement toward renewal and reform in the Church.

Deposit of the Faith: The body of saving truth, entrusted by Christ to the apostles and handed on by them to the Church to be preserved and proclaimed. As embodied in Revelation and Tradition the term is very nearly coextensive with objective revelation, in that it embraces the whole of Christ's teaching. But the term "deposit" highlights particular features of the apostolic teaching implying that this teaching is an inexhaustible store that rewards and promotes reflection and study so that new insights and deeper penetration might be made into the mystery of the divine economy of salvation. Although our understanding of this teaching can develop, it can never be augmented in its substance; the teaching is a divine trust, which cannot be altered, modified, or debased. The term *depositum fidei* first entered official Catholic teaching with the Council of Trent, but its substance is well-attested in the Scriptures and writings of the Fathers.

Dicastery: A broad term used for the various offices and departments of the Roman Curia.

Diocese: A particular church, a fully organized ecclesiastical jurisdiction under the pastoral direction of a bishop as local ordinary.

Ecclesiology: Study of the nature, constitution, members, mission, functions, etc., of the Church.

Ecumenism: The movement of Christians and their churches toward the unity willed by Christ. The Second Vatican Council called the movement "those activities and enterprises which, according to various needs of the Church and opportune occasions, are started and organized for the fostering of unity among Christians" (Decree on Ecumenism, No. 4). Spiritual ecumenism — that is, mutual prayer for unity — is the heart of the movement. The movement also involves scholarly and pew-level efforts for the development of mutual understanding and better interfaith relations in general, and collaboration by the churches and their members in the social area.

Encyclical: The highest form of papal teaching document. It is normally addressed to all the bishops and/or to all the faithful.

Episcopate: (1) The office, dignity, and sacramental powers bestowed upon a bishop at his ordination. (2) The body of bishops collectively.

Ethics: Moral philosophy, the science of the morality of human acts deriving from natural law, the natural end of man, and the powers of human reason. It includes all the spheres of human activity — personal, social, economic, political, etc. Ethics is distinct from but can be related to moral theology, whose primary principles are drawn from divine revelation.

Evangelization: Proclamation of the Gospel, the Good News of salvation in and through Christ, among those who have not yet known or received it; and efforts for the progressive development of the life of faith among those who have already received the Gospel and all that it entails. Evangelization is the primary mission of the Church, in which all members of the Church are called to participate.

Excommunication: A penalty or censure by which a baptized Catholic is excluded from the communion of the faithful, for committing and remaining obstinate in certain serious offenses specified in canon law; e.g., heresy, schism, apostasy, abortion. As by baptism a person is made a member of the Church in which there is a communication of spiritual goods, so by excommunication he is deprived of the same spiritual goods until he repents and receives absolution. Even though excommunicated, a person is still responsible for fulfillment of the normal obligations of a Catholic.

Fisherman's Ring: A signet ring (termed in Italian the *pescatorio*) engraved with the image of Saint Peter fishing from a boat, and encircled with the name of the reigning pope. It is not worn by the pope. It is used to seal briefs, and is destroyed after each pope's death.

General Congregation: The name used for the meetings of the cardinals in Rome that are held during the *sede vacante*. The purpose of the meetings is limited strictly to the preparations for the funeral of the deceased pope and the preparations for the conclave. The cardinals are not permitted to appoint new members to the College of Cardinals or set aside any provisions of the regulations under which the activities of the *sede vacante* are governed.

Hierarchy: The authorities of order who carry out the sacramental, teaching, and pastoral ministry of the Church; the hierarchy consists of the pope, bishops, priests, and deacons; the pope and the bishops give pastoral governance to the faithful.

Holy Father: A title used for the pope; it is a shortened translation of the Latin title *Beatissimus Pater*, "Most Blessed Father," and refers to his position as the spiritual father of all the Christian faithful.

Holy See: (1) The diocese of the pope, Rome. (2) The pope himself and/or the various officials and bodies of the Church's central administration at Vatican City — the Roman Curia — which act in the name and by authority of the pope.

Incardination: The affiliation of a priest to his diocese. Every secular priest must belong to a certain diocese. Similarly, every priest of a religious community must belong to some jurisdiction of his community; this affiliation, however, is not called incardination.

Infallibility: (1) The inability of the Church to err in its teaching, in that she preserves and teaches the deposit of truth as revealed by Christ. (2) The inability of the Roman pontiff to err when he teaches *ex cathedra* in matters of faith or morals, and indicates that the doctrine is to be believed by all the faithful. (3) The inability of the college of bishops to err when speaking in union with the pope in matters of faith and morals, agreeing that a doctrine must be held by the universal Church, and the doctrine is promulgated by the pontiff.

Inquisition: A tribunal for dealing with heretics, authorized by Gregory IX in 1231 to search them out, hear and judge them, sentence them to various forms of punishment, and in some cases to hand them over to civil authorities for punishment. The Inquisition was a creature of its time when crimes against faith, which threatened the good of the Christian community, were regarded also as crimes against the state, and when heretical doctrines of such extremists as the Cathari and Albigensians threatened the very fabric of society. The institution, which was responsible for many excesses, was most active in the second half of the thirteenth century.

Instruction: A document containing doctrinal explanations, directive norms, rules, recommendations, admonitions issued by the pope, a department of the Roman Curia, or other competent authority in the Church. To the extent that they so prescribe, instructions have the force of law.

Interdict: A censure imposed on persons for certain violations of Church law. Interdicted persons may not take part in certain liturgical services, administer or receive certain sacraments.

Jurisdiction: Right, power, authority to rule. Jurisdiction in the Church is of divine institution; has pastoral service for its purpose; includes legislative, judicial, and executive authority; can be exercised only by persons with the power of orders. (1) Ordinary jurisdiction is attached to ecclesiastical offices by law; the officeholders, called ordinaries, have authority over those who are subject to them. (2) Delegated jurisdiction is that which is granted to persons rather than attached to offices. Its extent depends on the terms of the delegation.

Keys, Power of the: Spiritual authority and jurisdiction in the Church, symbolized by the keys of the kingdom of heaven. Christ promised the keys to Saint Peter, as head-to-be of the Church (see Mt 16:19), and commissioned him with full pastoral responsibility to feed his lambs and sheep (Jn 21:15-17), The pope, as the successor of Saint Peter, has this power in a primary and supreme manner. The bishops of the Church also have the power, in union with and subordinate to the pope. Priests share in it through holy orders and the delegation of authority. Examples of the application of the Power of the Keys are the exercise of teaching and pastoral authority by the pope and bishops, the absolving of sins in the Sacrament of Penance, the granting of indulgences, the imposing of spiritual penalties on persons who commit certain serious sins.

Laicization: The process by which a man ordained to holy orders is relieved of the obligations of orders and the ministry and is returned to the status of a layperson.

Liberation Theology: Deals with the relevance of Christian faith and salvation — and, therefore, of the mission of the Church — to efforts for the promotion of human rights, social justice and human development. It originated in the religious, social, political, and economic environment of Latin America, with its contemporary need for a theory and corresponding action by the Church, in the pattern of its overall mission, for human rights and integral personal and social development. Some versions of liberation theology are at variance with the body of Church teaching because of their ideological concept of Christ as liberator, and also because they play down the primary spiritual nature and mission of the Church. Instructions from the Congregation for the Doctrine of the Faith — "On Certain Aspects of the Theology of Liberation" (September 3, 1984) and "On Christian Freedom and Liberation" (April 5, 1986) — contain warnings against translating sociology into theology and advocating violence in social activism.

Magisterium: The Church's teaching authority, instituted by Christ and guided by the Holy Spirit, which seeks to safeguard and explain the truths of the faith. The magisterium is exercised in two ways. The extraordinary magisterium is exercised when the pope and ecumenical councils infallibly define a truth of faith or morals that is necessary for one's salvation and that has been constantly taught and held by the Church. Ordinary magisterium is exercised when the Church infallibly defines truths of the Faith as taught universally and without dissent; which must be taught or the magisterium would be failing in its duty; is connected with a grave matter of faith or morals; and which is taught authoritatively. Not everything taught by the magisterium is done so infallibly; however, the exercise of the magisterium is faithful to Christ and what he taught.

Millennium: A thousand-year reign of Christ and the just upon earth before the end of the world. This belief of the Millenarians, Chiliasts, and some sects of modern times is based on an erroneous interpretation of Revelation 20.

Mission: (1) Strictly, it means being sent to perform a certain work, such as the mission of Christ to redeem mankind, the mission of the apostles and the Church and its members to perpetuate the prophetic, priestly and royal mission of Christ. (2) A place where the Gospel has not been proclaimed; the Church has not been firmly established; the Church, although established, is weak. (3) An ecclesiastical territory with the simplest kind of canonical organization, under the jurisdiction of the Congregation for the Evangelization of Peoples. (4) A church or chapel without a resident priest. (5) A special course of sermons and spiritual exercises conducted in parishes for the purpose of renewing and deepening the spiritual life of the faithful and for the conversion of lapsed Catholics.

Modernism: The "synthesis of all heresies," which appeared near the beginning of the twentieth century. It undermines the objective validity of religious beliefs and practices which, it contends, are products of the subconscious developed by mankind under the stimulus of a religious sense. It holds that the existence of a personal God cannot be demonstrated, the Bible is not inspired, Christ is not divine, nor did he establish the Church or institute the sacraments. A special danger lies in modernism, which is still influential, because it uses Catholic terms with perverted meanings. Saint Pius X condemned sixty-five propositions of modernism in 1907 in the decree *Lamentabili Sane* and issued the encyclical *Pascendi dominici gregis* to explain and analyze its errors.

Monastery: The dwelling place, as well as the community thereof, of monks belonging to the Benedictine and Benedictine-related orders like the Cistercians and Carthusians; also, the Augustinians and Canons Regular. Distinctive of monasteries are: their separation from the world; the enclosure or cloister; the permanence or stability of attachment characteristic of their members; autonomous government in accordance with a monastic rule, like that of Saint Benedict in the West or of Saint Basil in the East; the special dedication of its members to the community celebration of the liturgy as well as to work that is suitable to the surrounding area and the needs of its people. Monastic superiors of men have such titles as abbot and prior; of women, abbess and prioress. In most essentials, an abbey is the same as a monastery.

Motu Proprio: A Latin phrase designating a document issued by a pope on his own initiative. Documents of this kind often concern administrative matters.

Neo-Scholasticism: A movement begun in the late nineteenth century that had as its aim the restoration of Scholasticism for use in contemporary philosophy and theology. Great emphasis was placed upon the writings of such Scholastic masters as Peter Lombard, Saint Albert the Great, Saint Anselm, Saint Bonaventure, Blessed John Duns Scotus, and especially Saint Thomas Aquinas. The movement began at the Catholic University of Louvain, in Belgium, and then found its way into theological centers in Italy, France, and Germany. Particular attention was given to the philosophical and theological works of Saint Thomas Aquinas, from which arose a particular school of neo-Thomism; the movement was strongly reinforced by Pope Leo XIII who issued the encyclical *Aeterni Patris* (1879) mandating that Scholasticism, in particular Thomism, be the foundation for all Catholic philosophy and theology taught in Catholic seminaries, universities, and colleges. Neo-Scholasticism was responsible for a true intellectual renaissance in twentieth-century Catholic philosophy and theology. Among its foremost modern leaders were Jacques Maritain, Étienne Gilson, M. D. Chenu, Henri de Lubac, Yves Simon, and Paul Claudel.

Novemdiales: The nine days of official mourning that are held after the death of the pope. They are to take place sequentially during the period between the death of the pontiff and the start of the conclave.

Ordination: The consecration of sacred ministers for divine worship and the service of people in things pertaining to God. The power of ordination comes from Christ and the Church, and must be conferred by a minister capable of communicating it.

Pallium: A band of white wool worn over the shoulders by all metropolitan archbishops and the pope. The pallium is normally decorated with six black crosses and is made from the wool of two lambs blessed in the Church of Saint Agnes in Rome. It is a symbol of union with the Holy See. Pope John Paul I was invested with the pallium at his installation in 1978, and John Paul II adopted the custom. Pope Benedict XVI was invested with a pallium adorned with five red crosses (symbolizing the wounds of Christ).

Papabile (also Papabili, pl.): An Italian word meaning essentially, "popeable." It is used to describe a cardinal who is considered a strong possible candidate to become the next pope.

Papal Election: The pope is elected by the College of Cardinals during a secret conclave which begins no sooner than fifteen days and no later than twenty days after the death of his predecessor. Cardinals under the age of eighty, totaling no more than 120, are eligible to take part in the election by secret ballot. Election is by a two-thirds vote of participating cardinals.

Patriarchs: (1) The leaders of the Israelite tribes and heads of prominent families who appear in Genesis from Adam to Joseph. Among the most significant patriarchs of the Old Testament are Abraham, Isaac, and Jacob; the patriarchal narratives in Genesis associated with them constitute the prologue to Israel's salvation history, and the period during which they lived is known as the Age of the Patriarchs. It is to be noted that the title of patriarch that was used for David (see Acts 2:29) was simply one of honor. (2) The head of a branch of the Eastern Church, corresponding to a province of the one-time Roman Empire. There are five official traditional patriarchal sees: Rome, Constantinople, Alexandria, Antioch, and Jerusalem. Presently, the autocephalous churches of the Orthodox Church comprise several of these traditional patriarchates.

Pectoral Cross: A cross worn on a chain about the neck and over the breast by bishops and abbots as a mark of their office.

People of God: A name for the Church in the sense that it is comprised by a people with Christ as its head, the Holy Spirit as the condition of its unity, the law of love as its rule, and the kingdom of God as its destiny. Although it is a scriptural term, it was given new emphasis by the Second Vatican Council's Dogmatic Constitution on the Church (*Lumen Gentium*).

Pope: A title from the Italian word *papa* (from Greek *pappas*, father) used for the Bishop of Rome, the Vicar of Christ, and successor of Saint Peter, who exercises universal governance over the Church.

Relativism: Theory which holds that all truth, including religious truth, is relative — that is, not absolute, certain or unchanging; a product of agnosticism, indifferentism, and an unwarranted extension of the notion of truth in positive science. Relativism is based on the tenet that certain knowledge of any and all truth is impossible. Therefore, no religion, philosophy, or science can be said to possess the real truth; consequently, all religions, philosophies and sciences may be considered to have as much or as little of truth as any of the others.

Ring: In the Church a ring is worn as part of the insignia of bishops, abbots, et al.; by sisters to denote their consecration to God and the Church. The wedding ring symbolizes the love and union of husband and wife.

Rogito: The official notarial act or document testifying to the burial of a pope.

Scholasticism: The term usually applied to the Catholic theology and philosophy which developed in the Middle Ages.

Secularism: A school of thought, a spirit and manner of action which ignores and/or repudiates the validity or influence of supernatural religion with respect to individual and social life.

Sede Vacante: The Latin term, meaning "vacant see," that is used for the papal interregnum. During the *sede vacante*, all formal official business in the governance of the Church ceases and resumes again only after the election of the new pope. During the *sede vacante*, day-to-day administration of the Church is in the hands of the camerlengo and the College of Cardinals.

Seminary: A house of study and formation for men, called seminarians, preparing for the priesthood. Traditional seminaries date from the Council of Trent in the middle of the sixteenth century; before that time, candidates for the priesthood were variously trained in monastic schools, universities under church auspices, and in less formal ways.

Suspension: A censure by which a cleric is forbidden to exercise some or all of his powers of orders and jurisdiction, or to accept the financial support of his benefices.

Synod, Diocesan: Meeting of representative persons of a diocese — priests, religious, laypersons — with the bishop, called by him for the purpose of considering and taking action on matters affecting the life and mission of the Church in the diocese. Persons taking part in a synod have consultative status; the bishop alone is the legislator, with power to authorize synodal decrees. According to canon law, every diocese should have a synod every ten years.

Te Deum: The opening Latin words, *Thee, God*, of a hymn of praise and thanksgiving prescribed for use in the Office of Readings of the Liturgy of the Hours on many Sundays, solemnities, and feasts.

Theology: Knowledge of God and religion, deriving from and based on the data of divine revelation, organized and systematized according to some kind of scientific method. It involves systematic study and presentation of the truths of divine revelation in Sacred Scripture, tradition, and the teaching of the Church. Theology has been divided under various subject headings. Some of the major fields have been: dogmatic (systematic theology), moral, pastoral, historical, ascetical (the practice of virtue and means of attaining holiness and perfection), sacramental, and mystical (higher states of religious experience). Other subject headings include ecumenism (Christian unity, interfaith relations), ecclesiology (the nature and constitution of the Church), and Mariology (doctrine concerning the Blessed Virgin Mary), etc.

Thomism: The philosophy based on Saint Thomas Aquinas (1224/5-1274), which is mandated to be the dominant philosophy used in Catholic educational institutions.

Titular Sees: Dioceses where the Church once flourished but which now exist only in name or title. Bishops without a territorial or residential diocese of their own — for example, auxiliary bishops — are given titular sees. There are more than 2,000 titular sees; 16 of them are in the United States.

***Urbi et Orbi*:** A Latin phrase meaning "To the City and to the World" that is a blessing given by the Holy Father. Normally, the first *Urbi et Orbi* delivered by a pontiff is immediately after his election by the College of Cardinals. This is a blessing accompanied by a short address to the crowds in Saint Peter's Square and to the world; frequently, as with Pope John Paul II in 1978, it is delivered in as many languages as possible. The pope also delivers an *Urbi et Orbi* each year at Christmas and at Easter.

***Veni Creator Spiritus*:** A Latin phrase, meaning "Come, Creator Spirit," that is part of a hymn sung to the Holy Spirit. The hymn invokes the presence of the Holy Spirit and was perhaps first composed by Rabanus Maurus (776-856). The hymn is commonly sung as part of the Divine Office, papal elections, episcopal consecrations, ordinations, councils, synods, canonical elections, and confirmations.

Vocation: A call to a way of life. Generally, the term applies to the common call of all persons, from God, to holiness and salvation. Specifically, it refers to particular states of life, each called a vocation, in which response is made to this universal call: marriage, the religious life and/or priesthood, the single state freely chosen or accepted for the accomplishment of God's will. The term also applies to the various occupations in which persons make a living. The Church supports the freedom of each individual to choose a particular vocation, and reserves the right to pass on the acceptability of candidates for the priesthood and religious life. Signs or indicators of particular vocations are many, including a person's talents and interests, circumstances and obligations, invitations of grace and willingness to respond thereto.

Vow: A promise made to God with sufficient knowledge and freedom, which has as its object a moral good that is possible and better than its voluntary omission. A person who professes a vow binds himself or herself by the virtue of religion to fulfill the promise. The best-known examples of vows are those of poverty, chastity, and obedience professed by religious. Public vows are made before a competent person, acting as an agent of the Church, who accepts the profession in the name of the Church, thereby giving public recognition to the person's dedication and consecration to God and divine worship. Vows of this kind are either solemn, rendering all contrary acts invalid as well as unlawful; or simple, rendering contrary acts unlawful. Solemn vows are for life; simple vows are for a definite period of time or for life. Vows professed without public recognition by the Church are called private vows. The Church, which has authority to accept and give public recognition to vows, also has authority to dispense persons from their obligations for serious reasons.

Zucchetto: A small skullcap worn by ecclesiastics, most notably prelates, and derived from the popular Italian vernacular term *zucca*, meaning a pumpkin, and used as slang for head. The Holy Father wears a white zucchetto made of watered silk; cardinals use scarlet, and bishops use purple. Priests of the monsignorial rank may wear black with purple piping. All others may wear simple black.